IN THE HANDS OF THE ENEMY

BY THE SAME AUTHOR

AFRICAN MISSIONS. Impressions of the South, East, and Centre of the Dark Continent. Published by the S.P.C.K. 3s. 6d.

OUR OPPORTUNITY IN THE WEST INDIES. Published by the S.P.G. 1s.

THE METHOD OF THE STUDY CIRCLE. Published by the Lay Reader. 1d.

TO

MY FELLOW-PRISONERS

WHO ALREADY DURING TWELVE LONG MONTHS

HAVE BORNE

DISAPPOINTMENT WITH PATIENT RESIGNATION

AND INSULTS WITH SILENT DIGNITY

WHO HAVE MADE THE NAME OF BRITAIN RESPECTED

IN THE HEART OF GERMANY

AND WHO ARE

EMPLOYING THEIR PERIOD OF ENFORCED LEISURE AS A

PREPARATION FOR FUTURE USEFULNESS

THIS SHORT RECORD OF OUR INTERNMENT TOGETHER

IS AFFECTIONATELY DEDICATED BY

THE AUTHOR

The Coldstream Guards at Landrecies, 10 P.M. Aug. 25, 1914
From a Drawing by W. B. Wollen, R.I.

IN THE HANDS OF THE ENEMY

BEING THE EXPERIENCES OF A PRISONER OF WAR

BY

BENJAMIN G. O'RORKE, M.A.
CHAPLAIN TO THE FORCES

> "Wouldest thou smite those whom thou hast taken captive with thy sword and with thy bow? Set bread and water before them, that they may eat and drink."—2 KINGS vi. 22.

WITH ILLUSTRATIONS

The Naval & Military Press Ltd

Reproduced by kind permission of the Central Library,
Royal Military Academy, Sandhurst

Published by
The Naval & Military Press Ltd
Unit 10 Ridgewood Industrial Park,
Uckfield, East Sussex,
TN22 5QE England
Tel: +44 (0) 1825 749494
Fax: +44 (0) 1825 765701
www.naval-military-press.com
www.military-genealogy.com
www.militarymaproom.com

In reprinting in facsimile from the original, any imperfections are inevitably reproduced and the quality may fall short of modern type and cartographic standards.

PREFACE

It may be well to state that these reminiscences, such as they are, gain nothing in colouring from having been viewed as scenes of the past from the safe shores of England. Nor do they lose anything by reason of the darkening haze which unhappily at present hangs between Germany and this country. They were recorded day by day in Germany itself. It may therefore be claimed for them that they describe incidents in the mood and spirit in which they were experienced,—and that spirit, the writer believes, he caught from the British officers and men who shared his experiences. If he has accurately reflected it, it is a spirit of imperturbable optimism, and the relatives of prisoners of war will take heart accordingly. The British prisoners with whom the writer came into contact discern a silver lining in every cloud, and a touch of humour in any petty annoyance they meet with.

Nearly the whole of the diary on which this narrative is based was confiscated by the Germans when the writer was searched for the last time before his release, and was restored to him by post a few weeks later, bearing a mark that it had been passed by the Censor. He therefore regards himself as exempted from any compunction he might have felt in giving it this form of publicity.

Chap. x. originally appeared in *The Church Family Newspaper* and part of chap. xiii. in *The Daily Mail*.

CONTENTS

CHAP.		PAGE
I.	The Fateful Fourth	9
II.	Off to the Front	13
III.	The Battle of Landrecies	17
IV.	Prisoners!	27
V.	Torgau	32
VI.	The Journey to Burg	50
VII.	Burg: Settling In	58
VIII.	Burg: Settling Down	70
IX.	The Reprisal Prisoners	80
X.	On Parole	86
XI.	Torgau Revisited and Halle	89
XII.	Magdeburg	96
XIII.	Prison Occupations	105

LIST OF ILLUSTRATIONS

PLATES

		PAGE
THE COLDSTREAM GUARDS AT LANDRECIES	*Frontispiece*	
A GERMAN SENTRY DOING HIS BIT	*facing*	50
THE COMMANDANT AT BURG	,,	72
STUDIES IN HEADS	,,	80
THE WAGENHAUS, MAGDEBURG	,,	96
THE COMMANDANT AT MAGDEBURG AND HIS ADJUTANT	,,	100

IN THE TEXT

LANDRECIES	23
PLAN OF BRÜCKENKOPF, TORGAU	33
INTERIOR OF ST. LUKE'S CHAPEL, TORGAU	39
A GERMAN GUARD AND HIS GUARDIAN	43
OUR RUSSIAN FRIENDS GROW BEARDS, BUT AT DIFFERENT ELEVATIONS	59
THE OLD RUSSIAN COLONEL TAKING A CONSTITUTIONAL	61
A CAPTIVE RUSSIAN PRIEST	67
AT WORK AND AT PLAY	109

IN THE HANDS OF THE ENEMY

I.—THE FATEFUL FOURTH

THE by-ways of history have an interest of their own. They lack the romance and thrill and importance of the highways, it is true, nevertheless they have their place, just as a map, which marked the railways and leading thoroughfares, but left out the minor tracks and country lanes, would be manifestly incomplete. The following reminiscences are written primarily for the information of those who have friends interned as prisoners of war. Their secondary aim is to place on record, at the suggestion of some of my fellow-prisoners, a few of our experiences and the manner in which we spent our days of enforced idleness.

The state of war between England and Germany began at 11 P.M. on August 4, 1914, Tuesday "the fateful fourth." Everyone had heard so much about the inevitable conflict which never came, that they had begun to believe that it would never come. On August 12 I reported myself to Major P. H. Collingwood, R.A.M.C., the commanding officer of the 4th Field Ambulance, the unit to which I had been attached as Chaplain. It was destined to form part of the 2nd Division of the Expeditionary Force, and was then mobilising in Aldershot. It comprised three sections. Major Collingwood, assisted by Lieut. A. J. Brown, Lieut. J. Lauder, and Lieut. and Quartermaster L. Jones, commanded Section A. Captain J. P. Lynch, Lieut. S. M. Hattersley, and Lieut. H. Hills formed

Section B. And Section C was composed of Major P. H. Falkner, Captain A. A. Sutcliff, and Lieut. L. Routh. There were some 260 N.C.O.'s and men of the Royal Army Medical Corps, and a party of Army Service Corps drivers to look after the ambulance wagons and the horses. Our orders were to attach ourselves to the 4th (Guards) Brigade at the front, and to keep as much as possible to the sectional arrangement in case we had to part company on separate errands. I was posted to B Section for messing, and Pte. G. Whyman, of the Gloucester Regiment, an old and trusted friend, volunteered to come with me in the capacity of soldier servant and groom.

On Saturday, August 15, we entrained, whither we knew not. The railway officials either did not know or would not tell, but we were not long before we discovered that our destination was Southampton.

Here we spent a wearisome afternoon and evening at the docks, embarking horses and wagons on board our transport, a cattle-boat named *Armenian*, which has since been sunk by the Germans. With us embarked contingents of the 18th Hussars and 9th Lancers. It was a calm journey, and there were no signs of sea-sickness. Pipes and cigarettes were freely smoked, a good sign on the first day of a voyage. Once more our destination was kept a profound secret, even from the captain, until we got well out to sea. It being Sunday, we had a service on board, which gave me a golden opportunity of addressing my flock for the first time. Speaking on the text, "Whoso feareth the Lord shall not be afraid, and shall not play the coward," Ecclus. xxiv. 14 (R.V.), I reminded them that we were setting out to take our part in the greatest war in history. We would do well to carry with us a watchword—the word REMEMBER. We should remember first our country. Its share in the quarrel was an honourable one. We sought to acquire no fresh territory, to redress no private grievance. "Thrice arm'd is he that hath his quarrel just." Then, our country's glorious past. Our history was

THE FATEFUL FOURTH 11

like an immense regimental banner emblazoned with honours. That banner was placed in our hands to hold it aloft, to add to its record, and to preserve it from stains. There was, further, our country's standard of honour. We must so conduct ourselves that our foes should first respect the British flag and then come to love it, as in the case of the Boer War. Cruelty to the weak and helpless, and wanton destruction of property, were foreign to our national code. Secondly, we should remember the old folks at home, whose hardships in our absence might equal and even exceed our own. Finally, if we always remembered God, we should not fight the worse, we should fight and endure hardness all the better, never being "afraid" and never "playing the coward."

After the service on deck, a number of officers and men, after the example of the knights of old who consecrated their swords at the altar, partook of the Holy Communion in the saloon.

In the course of the afternoon we sighted the beautiful harbour of Boulogne, where we landed. "'Eep, 'eep, 'ooray!" called out the crowds of French people who lined the pier and landing-stage to give us a hearty welcome as their allies. From the first moment we were made to feel at home in France, and careful arrangements had been undertaken for our comfort. To every regiment a Frenchman was appointed as interpreter, many of whom were educated men of good standing. One regiment had as interpreter the French master at Blundell's School; the one allotted to the 4th Field Ambulance was named Bernard, a dentist.

Strolling through the town, I passed the barracks where the Argyll and Sutherland Highlanders were quartered. True to their national characteristic that "a Scotsman is never at home unless he is abroad," they appeared to have been at Boulogne for years, and already to be on intimate terms with the townsfolk. On the steps of the Post Office was a bareheaded woman in the act of posting a letter to her son at the front. She spoke to me about him very tenderly, and it was obvious that all sorts of good wishes and prayers were dropped into the letter-box with her letter. It was dark and getting late when the 4th Field Ambulance marched off to the camping ground at Marlborough Camp on the Calais Road, which we reached at two in the morning. It was situated alongside a tall monument not unlike the Nelson column in Trafalgar Square, erected in memory of the Legion of Honour and of Napoleon Bonaparte. By a coincidence its foundation-stone was laid on August 17, 1804, and our arrival was August 17, 1914.

The whole of that day being spent as a day of rest we had opportunity to look round the town. Issued as a poster was a letter from the Mayor of Boulogne which ran as follows:

"Appeal to the Inhabitants.

"MY DEAR CITIZENS,—This very day arrive in our town the valiant British troops, who come to co-operate with our brave soldiers to repel the abominable aggression of Germany. So before the invasion of the Barbarians all Europe rose against the like race (*la race germaine*) who menaced the peace of the world and the security of other people.

"Boulogne, which is one of the homes of the Entente Cordiale, will give to the sons of the United Kingdom an enthusiastic and brotherly welcome. The citizens are requested on this occasion to decorate the fronts of their houses with the colours of the two countries.

"At the Hotel de Ville, *Aug.* 10, 1914.
"Le Maire de Boulogne, FÉLIX ADAM."

Consequently flags were in evidence everywhere. Men wore in their button-holes the colours of France, Belgium, and England intertwined, and women pinned them to their dresses. Little children followed the soldiers about, crying, "Souvenir, souvenir!" and pointed

OFF TO THE FRONT

to their regimental badges. After a while it was a rare sight to meet a soldier with a badge, or a French woman or child without one. The sole distinguishing mark between one regiment and another was the design of the badge on cap and the initials of the regiment on shoulder-strap drawn in indelible pencil.

The next morning the march through the town to the station was little short of a triumphal procession. The most popular figure amongst us was a diminutive soldier boy of the R.A.M.C., Trumpeter Berry. Some of the French women were with difficulty restrained from rushing out to kiss him. The crowd around the station as we left, pressing against the railings beyond which they were not permitted to go, gave us a send-off as enthusiastic as the welcome had been. Keepsakes, charms, blessings, and prayers were bestowed upon us generously. "*Vive la France!*" we shouted from the railway carriages, and we heard, dying away in the distance, the hearty response, "*Vive l'Angleterre!*"

II.—OFF TO THE FRONT

ENTRAINING at 3 P.M. on Tuesday, August 18, early the next morning we were bundled out hurriedly at Wassigny. We spent a few hours in a field near the station, shaved, and breakfasted. The headquarters of the 2nd Division were in the village. We saw Sir Douglas Haig, and heard the news that General Grierson had died in the train a few days previously, of heart failure, on the journey from Boulogne. The loss which that distinguished soldier's death involved to the army would have been great at any time; it was doubly so at the moment when it occurred.

9.30 A.M. found us marching to our first camping ground, Groucis, where we spent the nights of August 19 and 20. The headquarters of the Field Ambulance were the outbuildings of a farm. In the chamber adjoining our mess-room stayed Brig.-Gen. R. Scott-Kerr,

14 IN THE HANDS OF THE ENEMY

commanding the 4th (Guards) Brigade, which was also billeting in Groucis. Early on Friday, the 21st, we were on the march again in three separate sections, with intent to supply the place of two Field Ambulances which were not yet in the country. That night we halted at the village of La Groise. Major Falkner, Captain Sutcliff, Lieut. Routh and I billeted, the four of us together, in a bedroom of a farm-house. The men were accommodated in the barn and stables. At about 2 A.M. on Saturday we were aroused by an orderly with the news that the advance guard of our Division was in touch with the enemy near Mons. Great was our excitement. Lieut. Routh was at once despatched to arrange for billets at Pont-sur-Sambre, and in an hour or two the remainder of the section followed him. We formed the tail of the 5th Brigade, which included the Worcesters, the Connaught Rangers, and the Oxford and Bucks L.I. Our route passed through Landrecies, a little town which we were soon to know more intimately, and on the way, amongst other officers and men, I made the acquaintance of Lieut.-Col. A. Abercrombie, of the Connaught Rangers, and of Captain P. Godsal, Oxford and Bucks L.I., an acquaintance which was soon to ripen into friendship under different conditions in Germany. At Pont-sur-Sambre we were well received by the peasants at our billeting station. Eggs, fruit, cheese, milk, and vegetables were freely distributed amongst the men, tired out after a long march under a hot sun. It was here that we first heard the distant boom of guns, and were made aware that the fray had begun. In the evening I strolled into the town to make a few purchases for those whose duties kept them to the billeting area. Chocolate could not be had for love or money, but I managed to procure a few articles from the chemist's wife—evidently for love, not money. The good soul had a son at the front, and nothing would persuade her to take money, and in addition she gave me a sacred charm such as the French soldiers wear attached to their identification discs around their necks.

OFF TO THE FRONT

At 2.30 the next morning orders came to move off at 1.30 A.M.! The messenger had lost his way, and failed to reach us earlier. We bore him no grudge for this, however, for we were in ample time to drop into our place on the line of march, and we were fortified by an extra hour of sleep, which we badly needed before the day was out. It was a strange Sunday, to be marching off thus before daylight; it was also a memorable Sunday, for it was the day of the battle of Mons.

There was some uncertainty as to where we were required, and a good deal of the ground was covered thrice advancing, retiring, and advancing again. That morning we crossed the border into Belgium, and we took it as a good omen that our route passed through the battlefield of Malplaquet, and that it was Sunday, the day of the week on which Waterloo was fought. It was a hot and tiring march for horses and men who had had no breakfast. Haversack rations were eaten after we had been five or six hours on the dusty road. At 2.30 P.M. we reached Quevy-le-Grand. Sounds of artillery fire were quite distinct, aeroplanes were flying overhead, and our men stood on the tops of the ambulance wagons watching the shells burst, more calmly than if they were looking on at a football match. The tall tower of a sugar factory, a few miles south-west of Mons, was straight in front of us. The German shells seemed to be directed towards it or thereabouts, and our own shells appeared to issue from two directions in reply. The general opinion was, of course, that our gunners were forcing the Germans to retire.

At this point we were interrupted by the arrival of Colonel H. N. Thompson, D.S.O., A.D.M.S., to harangue the men. He had them drawn up informally, and from horseback read out Sir John French's letter to the troops. He added a few words of his own, exhorting them to reflect honour upon their Royal Corps, an admonition which they greeted with a rousing cheer.

After dark three ambulance wagons and all the

stretcher-bearers of C Section, under Captain Sutcliff and Lieut. Routh, were sent off to pick up some wounded men and an officer of the Irish Guards. The rest of us were to be ready to move when they came back. We lay down to sleep in a field just as we were, with wagons inspanned and horses saddled. Bovril was kept warm on the fire for the wounded when they came in. Before we lay down we had extemporised a hospital in a barn, covering the floor with a thick layer of straw in lieu of blankets.

The wounded did not in the end arrive, so we had the night undisturbed. With dawn came the news that the British losses on the previous day had been severe. One regiment was said to have only one officer and 50 men left, and another to have lost 400. The actual losses are now well known, but we were at that time dependent upon conflicting rumours and rough guesses.

Orders came to us that we were to retire from Quevy back again to Pont-sur-Sambre. This journey was unspeakably sad. The Belgians in the villages through which we passed had already begun to flee into France for protection. A long line of refugees marched with us, carrying such of their worldly goods as they could snatch up at the last moment. There were white-haired old men being wheeled along in barrows, cripples limping as fast as they could go, hatless women with a heavy bundle in one arm and an infant in the other, and by their side were two or three little toddlers wondering what it was all about. Behind were the homes with all their associations of the past and with the last meal, perhaps, still on the table untouched, so suddenly had the warning come. When would they see those homes again? If ever, probably as a heap of ruins. And in front, whither should they go? What had the future in store for them? "And all this misery," as an officer remarked, "under the cloudless sky of a brilliant summer's day— truly a contrast in light and shade." If those innocent souls merely looked back on the happy past and forward on the seemingly blank future, then their lot must indeed have been hopeless. We may be confident that they also looked up. Along the road they would have constant reminders that there was One above who knew all about it, and would not leave them comfortless. For at irregular intervals by the roadside in Belgium and France there are "Calvaries," little sanctuaries containing a figure of the Crucified One, seeming to whisper to all who pass by, "I have trodden this path before you."

III.—THE BATTLE OF LANDRECIES

A LONG march brought us back to Pont-sur-Sambre. We encamped in a field on the opposite side of the town to that in which we had been billeted on Saturday night. A peaceful night was welcome after the forced marches of the past few days. The sun was well up before we set out on Tuesday, August 25. Southwards again our direction lay; a strategic retirement, we were told. Early in the evening we reached Landrecies. Hardly had we passed the outskirts of the town before a scare arose. Civilians came tearing out of Landrecies. Motor cars and carts rushed past us at breakneck speed. The cry went up, "*Les Allemands!*" ("The Germans!"). A certain peasant who for the moment had lost control of himself whipped the horse which he was driving into a gallop, deaf to the heartrending call of some children who ran in panic after him begging him to give them a lift. Out rushed a footsore guardsman from one of the ambulance wagons, placed a rifle at his head, and compelled him to stop and pick them up.

None of us believed that there was any foundation for the scare. The Germans surely were miles away. Nevertheless we turned round and outspanned the wagons in a field a mile or two outside the town until

18 IN THE HANDS OF THE ENEMY

the road should be clear for us to march into it. We knew that the Guards Brigade was in Landrecies, and we expected that we should be summoned if and when we were wanted. There we remained until midnight. Long before that hour we became aware that the rumour was correct. At about 8 P.M. we heard the rat-a-tat-tat of machine guns and the boom of field artillery. The men of the Royal Army Medical Corps meanwhile awaited the summons that did not come. The rain came down in torrents, and they lay down wherever they could find a sheltered spot. Sleep for most of us was impossible. The din of battle was terrific. At last Major Collingwood decided to make a move. We were useless and possibly in danger where we lay. We might be of use if we proceeded. But whither? There was nothing to indicate the point from which the firing came. Was it at Maroilles, which lay behind us, or at Landrecies which lay in front? First we marched a mile in the direction of Maroilles. Then we reversed and turned towards Landrecies. At a corner on the outskirts of the town the Major detailed Lieut. Hattersley to remain there with some forty stretcher-bearers in the hope that they might prove of service. The remainder marched southwards to join up with the Guards Brigade at dawn, in the event of their following another road than that at which the stretcher-bearers were posted. I remained with Lieut. Hattersley. As the night wore on the firing became intermittent. Then we heard the heavy roll of gun carriages and the tramp of hoofs. The Brigade was evidently pursuing the direction taken by Major Collingwood. At dawn we moved on and caught up our main body.

A few hours later our line of march converged into the road along which the Landrecies troops were retreating. They were retreating because to do so was part of the scheme for the long line of which they were but a small section. They were retreating, but they had given a good account of themselves, and had the satisfaction of feeling that they had kept the Germans

THE BATTLE OF LANDRECIES 19

at bay against heavy odds. First in the procession came the artillery. They gave a cheerful account of the engagement. Only one battery—the 9th—had been in action, but they felt that they had done what they had been expected to do. Then came the Guards Brigade, marching bravely but very wearily. When the Brigade Major saw us, he asked us to return to Landrecies to tend the sick and wounded, of which the Coldstream Guards estimated that they had about 140. Colonel G. P. Feilding, the commanding officer, asked me to look out for Lord Hawarden, who he feared was mortally wounded, and Major T. G. Matheson hurriedly pencilled a note for the Hon. Rupert Keppel, who had also been hit.

The Germans were just on the point of taking over Landrecies when we returned thither, arriving at about 8 A.M. We at once made for the building which served as a hospital, where a mournful sight awaited us. The bodies of six or seven who had been killed were lying on stretchers, reverently covered over with blankets, in a quiet corner of the compound. Inside the building wounded men lay on beds and stretchers in every available space in the hall, the passages, and the rooms. As we entered at the gate one or two ambulances, under the direction of Major Falkner, were carrying away such of the wounded as were fit to be removed; and they were fortunate enough to get away from the town before it was occupied by the Germans. Part of the 19th Field Ambulance, with Major W. B. Fry, Major J. J. Furness, Captain W. Beaman, and Lieut. A. B. Preston, had been in the town all night, and these medical officers were now busily engaged in dressing wounds and performing operations.

I went at once in search of the Hon. Rupert Keppel and handed to him Major Matheson's note. He was in an upstairs room with five or six wounded men. He was lying on a bed with a bandage round his forehead, but made light of the wounds which he had received. After a few words and a short prayer at each bedside, I made inquiries for Lord Hawarden. I was told that he was already dead, but I found him in a little room by himself, still breathing although apparently unconscious. He had lost his left arm, and a portion of his back had been shot away. I knelt down beside him and commended him to God, saying in the form of a prayer as from himself the hymn "Abide with me." As I rose from my knees he opened his eyes and smiled. He had been asleep merely, and now began to speak with quite a strong voice. Not a word did he say about himself or his sufferings. He talked about the battle, about his old home near Bordon, which was within a couple of miles of my own home and formed a happy link between us, and about his mother. On account of the nature of his wounds I considered it inexpedient to allow him to talk for any length of time. In a few minutes he fell asleep again.

The other poor patients were terribly knocked about. Limbs in some cases had been entirely blown off by shells. Lyddite had turned many complexions to a jaundiced yellow. And yet every man was calm and resigned, and proud to have had a share in the fight. The medical officers were going about their work in a skilful and business-like way as if it were an everyday task, and hardly a groan escaped from the men lying about on all sides, although many of the latter must have been in agony. A kindly French priest was going from bed to bed saying comforting words in French. Probably not one of the patients understood his words, but they all understood and appreciated his meaning. The orderlies, too, were untiring in their particular duties, worn out as many of them were by long marches, and lack of food and sleep. It was with no ordinary pleasure that I noticed amongst them an old friend, Sergeant-Major Mendel, R.A.M.C., with whom I had been brought into intimate touch at Aldershot and in South Africa years before.

THE BATTLE OF LANDRECIES 21

Meanwhile the Germans began to appear on the canal bridge near the hospital. Major Collingwood went out to meet them, and they entered the hospital with him. The officer in charge of them, Herr Ruttner of Berlin, shook hands with me and said that my work would not be interfered with, and that I had his permission to go anywhere over the scene of battle in search of the killed, and that I might bury them where most convenient. He said he was personally acquainted with Sir Douglas Haig, who with Sir John French had actually been in Landrecies the previous afternoon. He seemed disappointed not to find Sir Douglas there still, and desired to be remembered to him. By his orders the hospital was examined and all arms and ammunition were removed. A sentry was then placed at the gate. We will leave him there for the time being, and go back to the story of the battle of Landrecies as described to me by those who took an active part in the engagement.

The Guards Brigade arrived at Landrecies at about noon on Tuesday, August 25. They were at once distributed in billets and told that they would probably remain in the town until midnight. The French, who until then had occupied the town, continued their retirement, leaving it to be held by the 2nd Division. That afternoon, as already stated, Sir John French and Sir Douglas Haig were reported to have visited the town, and their presence within it appears to have been known to the Germans, which would account for the unexpected attack which they launched against it.

At about 5 P.M., while the Guards were enjoying a few hours' rest after their forced marches, a crowd of panic-stricken French women came rushing past from the upper end of the town, crying out that the Germans were at hand and would kill them. It was but the work of a few minutes before each company was lying across a street with fixed bayonets, "ready," as one of them expressed it, "to massacre as many Germans as might care to put in an appearance." After ten minutes' excitement it transpired that the alarm had no foundation, and that the Germans were miles away. Back they all trooped to their billets.

As a precaution it was thought desirable to send out two companies of the Coldstream Guards, under Captain Monck, to the Bavay Road entrance to the town, the direction from which the alarm had come. It now began to rain in torrents, accompanied by thunder. At 6.45 P.M. the thunder of a cannonade became audible a mile or two outside the town. Half an hour later the order was given for a third company of the Coldstream Guards to go out and relieve one of those already on outpost. They reached the extreme limit of the town, where a branch of the road leads—almost at right angles—in the direction of Le Cateau; at this point there was a pool of water. Here a barrier of men had been stretched across the road in two ranks, with a machine gun at either end. Except for some wire entanglements a short distance to the front the road was not barricaded.

Presently the rumbling of wheels and the thud of horse-hoofs could be heard approaching along the Bavay Road. A peasant woman came forth from one of the farmhouses near by and asked in a voice choked with sobs whether the Germans were near. She was told that it was either British troops or French; and the soldiers did their best to reassure the poor soul.

Nearer and nearer came the rumbling wheels. Captain Monck challenged in French and stepped out a few paces to make sure he was face to face with friends. "*Amis*," "*Français*," had been the answer to his challenge, in perfect French. "Good! Just one more question to make certain." Then, after a short pause, the Germans—for so it proved—charged forward, and Captain Monck was just in time to get back among his own men. The German charge was met by the concentrated fire of a machine gun and forty rifles.

In half a minute silence reigned. The enemy had

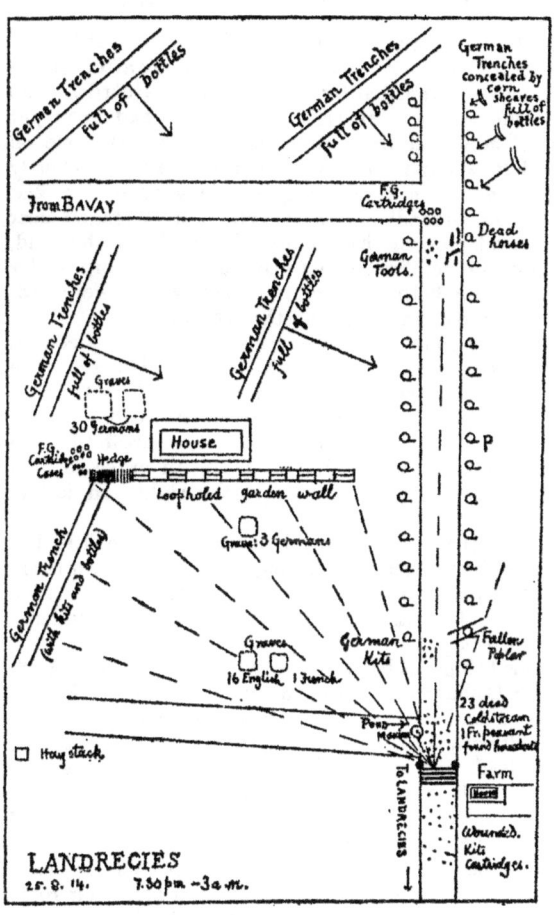

FROM A PLAN DRAWN FROM MEMORY BY CAPT. THE HON.
R. O. D. KEPPEL, COLDSTREAM GUARDS

24 IN THE HANDS OF THE ENEMY

withdrawn to prepare for a fresh attack. They had evidently been taken by surprise. Charge after charge was met and repelled by the Coldstream Guards. The machine gun on the right of the line had been put out of action at the commencement, but the one on the left wrought deadly execution, and was shortly reinforced by a machine gun belonging to the 2nd Battalion Grenadier Guards, who were engaged near the level crossing half a mile lower down the road. Meanwhile reinforcements had been drawn up under cover along both sides of the road, which were protected by barricades hastily thrown up.

All this time the Germans seem to have been in ignorance of the formation which opposed them. The blaze of a haystack set on fire revealed it to their eyes—a thin line stretching across the road. Thereupon they commenced to enfilade it, necessitating the retirement of this handful of troops in order to gain the protection of the walls to the right and left of them.

The German artillery did not long remain idle, but shelled simultaneously the piquet and the town itself. The battle thus raged with but little intermission until about 3 A.M., when the firing ceased as suddenly as it had begun.

This brings us back to the point where we left off. Major Collingwood having made arrangements for the housing and comfort of the wounded sent off Captain Sutcliff with a party of men to search for any wounded and dead who might still be lying where they fell. Let Captain Sutcliff himself tell the story in his own graphic manner:

"We began to search the town. One house I entered had been completely gutted, everything taken or destroyed. Many of the houses had half their roofs taken off by shells, and there were barricades of paving stones, pianos, bits of wood, and everything one could think of thrown up by the Guards. As we went up the street leading to the Bavay Road we ran into the

THE BATTLE OF LANDRECIES 25

German staff. They were civil enough, and after a time I got a pass signed allowing us to bury the dead, and to return after completion to the hospital at Landrecies.

"We went on up the street, right to the end. The sight there I shall never forget. From the bridge all the way up we had been treading on cartridges, but here there were literally tens of thousands lying about. Ammunition boxes with the lids torn off and only a dozen cartridges taken, canvas bandoliers full, broken rifles, pieces of equipment, packs, entrenching tools, and broken bayonets—and the dead! At first these were mostly in the left hedge, but just as we got to the open country there were twenty, all in twelve yards of road. They lay in all sorts of attitudes, just as they had died, arms half-extended and fists clenched. The injuries were awful. One man had five holes through his Pay Book in his breast-pocket. They had used thousands of cartridges which were lying around them. We found twenty-four dead altogether, all Coldstream except one French peasant.

"I went up the road and found a good many German kits in the ditch, and about 200 yards away the bodies of several horses. The road was bordered by poplars, and up to a height of about twenty feet the stems were riddled with rifle fire. Just beyond the houses was a pile of German field-gun cartridges, and some German spades very long and narrow in the blade. The German trenches were littered with bottles; apparently the German soldier had had a couple of bottles of wine to keep up his spirits in the trench. The red brick wall about 100 yards from the top of the road had been loopholed, and they had even put in rough seats behind. The work obviously took some time, and the Germans must have been at it all the time of the false alarm of the day before.

"The house behind the wall was spattered with bullets, and so was the wall itself. The people of the house were indoors, looking very white and scared, and

26 IN THE HANDS OF THE ENEMY

a large dog in the garden was utterly cowed. At the back we found two German graves, which accounted for thirty of them, their names being written up in indelible pencil on wooden crosses.

"We lowered the dead into the long grave which we had dug, and the Padre read the burial service. I made a rough cross about six feet by two feet out of some palings, and after putting it up we filled in the grave and marched back to hospital."[1]

It should be added that we found three bodies of German soldiers which had been overlooked by their friends. We gave them the same funeral rites as to our own comrades, and marked the place with a cross inscribed with their names.

In the early morning of the next day, Thursday, August 27, the gallant young Lord Hawarden died. The medical officer who looked after him said that he had never met a braver patient. A party of twelve men, under the command of Lieut. Hattersley, went with me to lay him to rest, together with the two officers and men whose bodies had been placed in the compound of the hospital as already described. We selected the best spot in the pretty little cemetery of Landrecies. In the first grave we placed Lord Hawarden and the Hon. A. Windsor Clive, of the Coldstream Guards. In the next grave Lieut. R. H. M. Vereker, Grenadier Guards. Next to that again, in one long grave, rest Privates W. Cox, T. Robson, R. Wells, G. Stainthorpe, B. Westcott, H. Slim, B. Watkins, of the Coldstream Guards, and Private J. Lander of the Gloucester Regiment. In two single graves alongside, later in the day, we placed a German soldier, and Private Tidy, Coldstream Guards, who died of wounds.

---

[1] A list of those buried on that occasion was given to a representative of the regiment, but a copy of it is not at present available for insertion in this narrative.

A few months later Captain Sutcliff's career came to an untimely end in circumstances as brave as those which he so vividly describes. He contracted typhus with fatal results, while attending prisoners of war in Germany.

The ceremony on each occasion concluded with a short space of silent prayer on behalf of the bereaved ones at home, that they might have strength given them to bear the blow when the news should reach them.

Before we left the cemetery a kindly Frenchwoman brought us a beautiful wooden cross to mark the spot. It was her tribute of gratitude to the men who had fought to save her town and home. We inscribed the names on it, and left instructions for the graves to be carefully tended after we were gone.

IV.—PRISONERS!

WE remained in Landrecies until Saturday, August 29, expecting daily to be returned to our own people in accordance with the terms of the Geneva Convention. Our destination, however, was fated to be in the opposite direction. Under an escort of half a dozen German soldiers, commanded by an under-officer, we marched out of the town, up the hill where the battle had taken place, to Bavay. It was a tiring journey for the wounded men lying in ambulance wagons. The Hon. R. Keppel was the only wounded officer. He travelled in a wagon with certain men of his regiment, with whom he appeared to be on exceedingly friendly terms. Two of the occupants of that wagon had lost an arm each, and they were the cheeriest of our party.

It was dark when we reached Bavay, and everyone was tired out. The journey seemed to be quite twenty miles. The first thing we did was to see the wounded safely into the hospital, which was a young men's college. M. L'Abbé J. Lebrun, the Superior, and his colleague were at the door to welcome us. I was at once taken into the English ward, and arrived just in time to commend the soul of a dying man, a private of the 12th Lancers. His officer—though wounded—had got out of bed to see the last of him, and besought me as I entered to visit his dying comrade without delay. His anxiety on his friend's behalf was a touching sight.

On the morrow, Sunday, August 30, I held a service, at the request of the patients, in the English ward. I spoke on "Be of good cheer," or, as we had so often heard it put by our French friends along the road, "*Bon courage.*" I gave the same address later on in the day to the R.A.M.C. men of the Field Ambulance and the convalescents, at a service held in the college refectory.

At the funeral of the 12th Lancer that afternoon we had an imposing procession. The body was laid on a stretcher covered over with a Union Jack and the French national flag. I led the way before the coffin, robed in a cassock and surplice which had been presented to me by a French priest to replace my own lost robes. After the coffin came the three R.C. priests of the town and a number of the French Red Cross nurses; then Major Collingwood and the men of the 4th Field Ambulance. One of the nurses, noticing that I had no stole, on returning from the funeral made me one of black material with three white crosses, and presented it within a couple of hours.

It should be mentioned that there was a ward in the hospital filled entirely with German wounded soldiers. They were accorded the same kindly treatment as was given to the British and French. Prince Reginald de Croy, who spoke English perfectly, seemed to be spending all his time amongst the patients, ministering with words of comfort to the wounded of all the nationalities.

The next day we were marched under escort to Mons. This is a large, well-built town of about 35,000 inhabitants. We were paraded through the cobbled streets to the barracks, then (evidently by a mistake) to the station, and finally back again to the barracks, where, in some dirty rooms over a filthy stable, we spent the night. Here we met the Hon.

Ivan Hay, of the 5th Lancers, who had narrowly escaped being shot after his capture by the Germans, but he was not allowed to accompany our party. The following morning we were marched once more to the station, and were bundled into the stationmaster's office, which was littered with looted papers. The men meanwhile were herded in a shed. A sentry was posted at the entrance of the station to prevent anyone going to the town. Just outside the station were the ambulance wagons and our servants. Whyman, my soldier-servant, was amongst them with my horse. That was the last I saw of either of them. I parted from them with a very sad heart.

During the afternoon an ill-mannered under-officer bade us hand over knives, razors, and sticks. At 6 P.M. we were entrained with about 1000 wounded, of whom some forty or fifty were ours, the rest being Germans. The train must have been a quarter of a mile long. In the middle of the night we passed through Brussels, and in the early morning through Louvain and Liége. Louvain seemed to be a heap of ruins; hardly a house visible from the station was intact. Here it was that, in 1516, Sir Thomas More published his "Utopia." How far from a Utopia, from an ideal earthly paradise, did it look now. "It is not possible," wrote More significantly, "for all things to be well unless all men are good; which I think will not be yet these many years." We looked with great interest upon Liége as we passed through it, and recalled the gallant defence of the town by the Belgians. A few more miles brought us over the border into Germany.

At Aachen a hostile demonstration took place at our expense. There happened to be a German troop train in the station at the time. A soldier of our escort displayed a specimen of the British soldier's knife, holding it up with the marline-spike open, and declared that this was the deadly instrument which British medical officers had been using to gouge out the eyes of the wounded Germans who had fallen into their vindictive hands! From the knife he pointed to the medical officers sitting placidly in the train, as much as to say, "And these are some of the culprits." This was too much for the German soldiers. They strained like bloodhounds on the leash. "Out with them!" said their irate colonel, pointing with his thumb over his shoulder to the carriages in which these bloodthirsty British officers sat. The colonel, however, did not wait to see his behest carried out, and a very gentlemanly German subaltern quietly urged his men to get back to their train and leave us alone. The only daggers that pierced us were the eyes of a couple of priests, a few women and boys, who appeared to be shocked beyond words that even a clergyman was amongst such wicked men. The enormity of the crimes which had necessitated my capture I could only conjecture from their looks.

At Düsseldorf we crossed the Rhine—a beautiful sight. At Essen I was permitted to visit one of our wounded men who was dying of tetanus. The unfortunate patients lay in rows on the floor of luggage vans, with straw beneath them. When the train stopped at a station the doors of these vans were sometimes flung open in order that the crowd might have a look at them.

At Dortmund, which we reached at about 8 on the following morning, we got out and were marched off to interview an officer who took down particulars about us. At Landrecies there had joined us Lieut. P. P. Butler, R.A.M.C., who could speak German fluently. On this occasion and during the whole time of our captivity he proved an invaluable asset to us. He had lived many years in Germany, and understood the national traits. His unresentful courtesy in his office as interpreter was largely responsible for such respect and consideration as we received. Hitherto we had failed to obtain any food or refreshment from German hands. Even the Red Cross ladies at the stations had steeled their hearts against us,

PRISONERS! 31

giving us not so much as a cup of coffee or a piece of bread. But for the haversack rations and chocolate, which most of us carried with us, we should have fared badly. Now, however, we were to receive our first meal from our captors. This consisted of a plate of hot soup and a slice of bread and butter, which we ate ravenously. Two kind ladies brought us this food, and we were duly grateful. One of them was standing near me as we ate the meal, and I thanked her cordially in English. She paid no attention, so I asked her if she understood English. "I do, but I don't mean to," was her laconic reply, which seemed highly to amuse my companions.

Tuesday, Wednesday, and Thursday, September 1, 2, and 3, were spent in that train. A second-class corridor coach was set apart for officers. How the men fared, and where they parted from us, we did not know. In the lavatory compartment there was hardly any water to wash with, and such food as we had with us soon began to run short. Eventually at two of the stopping-places we were allowed to get out and buy a meal at the station refreshment-room. On the journey one or two of us shaved, with the safety razor that was left to us, but the majority thought it would strike shame into the German inhabitants if they were to see us unshaven. We certainly must have looked a very interesting party from their point of view.

An officer, Lieut. M. C. Young, Duke of Wellington's (W. Riding) Regiment, afterwards related to us an amusing incident which occurred to him on a similar journey as a prisoner of war. When asked his name by the Germans, he replied innocently, "Young, of the Duke of Wellington's." To his surprise he found himself the recipient of unwonted attentions, a motor car being placed at his disposal and an officer told off to escort him. Not until afterwards did he learn the reason: the Germans had understood him to say that he was the "young Duke of Wellington." It was too late, however, when all the mischief was done, to make any explanations.

At length, on Friday morning, the journey came to an end on our arrival at Torgau. We were ordered out of the train and drawn up on the platform in fours. Each officer carried what articles of clothing he possessed. Several of them had preserved their medical panniers, and, heavy as these were, they had to be carried or left behind. On either side of us a German guard with fixed bayonets was drawn up, and then was given the word, "Quick march!" With our bundle on our shoulder, there was no man could be bolder, yet this same bundle and the burning sun prevented there being anything "quick" about our march. The townsfolk evidently had heard that we were coming, and they were at the station gate in scores to show us how pleased they were to welcome us to their town. In fact, they told us quite freely what they thought of us and the nation which we represented. They walked beside us every inch of the way, keeping up our spirits by telling us the particular kind of *Schweinhunds* they believed the *Engländer* to be. Not until they had crossed the massive bridge which spans the Elbe and reached the Brückenkopf fortress did they turn back home, and the doors of the fortress closed behind us.

V.—TORGAU

TORGAU is a Slav word meaning market. The town bearing that name has many historical associations. It figures in a document dating back to 973. In the Thirty Years War a portion of it was burnt. Amongst the distinguished names connected with it are Frederick the Great and Martin Luther. A statue of the former adorns one of its streets, and the Schloss on the opposite side of the river is inseparably bound up with the career of the latter. For in Luther's time a meeting was held there which decided upon the dialect into which the Bible was to be translated. Torgau, therefore, can be considered the cradle of the German Bible, and conse-

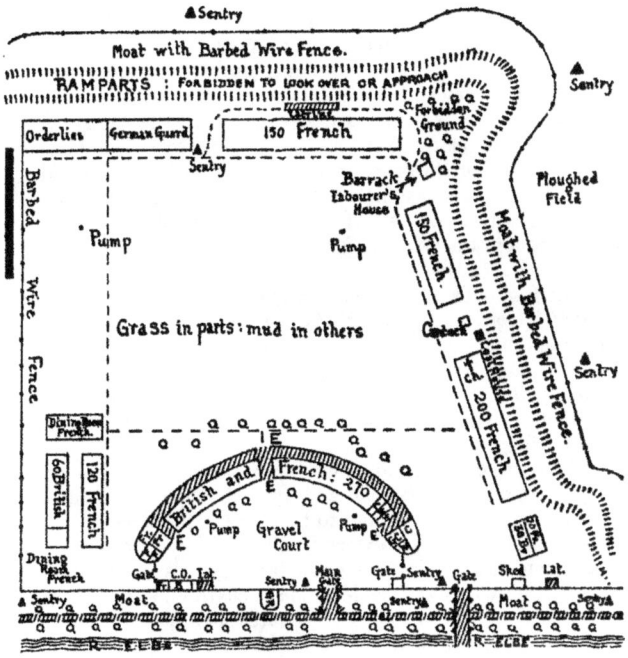

PLAN OF BRÜCKENKOPF, TORGAU

After a sketch by Lieut. J. E. T. Younger, R.F.A.

This plan is roughly to scale.
The black line on left edge of plan is the German shell store.
Dotted lines – – – – are paths.
In crescent-shaped building and sheds the letters are:

F—Quarters of French Generals.	Ch—St. Luke's Chapel.
Fr—Quarters allocated to French.	K—Kitchen.
B—Quarters allocated to British.	GC—German Commandant's Office.
C—Canteen.	E—Archway entrances.

On the line by Main Gate:
   CO—British Senior Officers' Qrs. | GR—German Guard Room.
                QQ—Trees.

The fort is approached by a bridge over the Elbe, thus

C

quently that of the national tongue. Luther himself visited the town at least forty times. In a house in Torgau Luther, Melancthon, and two others issued the "Torgau Articles," which became the basis of the Augsburg Confession. In April, 1811, the King of Saxony, Frederick August, the ally of Napoleon, destroyed the fortifications of the town in order to rebuild them. The reconstructed fortress is the one we are about to enter. On one of its stones, over the coal-house, the monogram of its founder is still decipherable, "F. A. R. 1812."

Passing over the moat through two iron doors, we enter a courtyard, about 100 yards long by 40 broad. Facing the gateway is a semi-circular building two storeys high, with an entrance at either end and one in the centre. A turret with windows and battlements surmounts each entrance; and from the central turret rises a flag-pole.

When we marched in on Friday, September 4, we found that a number of British and French officers had preceded us. There seemed to be about a hundred in all, of whom less than half were British. They were standing about in small groups, or sitting on stools, or strolling up and down, some hatless, some coatless, and one or two with an arm in a sling. Whatever they were doing, they stood stock-still with astonishment when our disreputable party entered and formed up in the centre of the court. They looked from the red-cross band upon our sleeves to the bayonets which bristled on the end of our escort's rifles, as though to say, "Who expected to see *you* here?"

Whilst we stood thus a young man with spectacles, dark blue trousers, and a soldier's khaki jacket entered our ranks and jotted down our names. We wondered who he could be. We learnt afterwards that this was Corporal Belfour, R.E., *alias* Prof. A. O. Belfour, M.A., of Eton, Christ Church, Oxford, and Queen's University, Belfast, who was acting as interpreter. Without his presence as "go-between" and his genial companionship in the days which lay before us, we should often have been at a loss.

We were next led off to our rooms. The one in which the majority of us were at first quartered was a spacious barrack-room on the upper floor, to the left of the semicircular building. Down the centre were two large tables. On the left, a cupboard or locker with shelves and pegs. On the right, twelve beds in tiers of two, one above the other, like the berths in a cabin. Two bowls, large and small, and a towel were allotted to each occupant.

Depositing our belongings here, we went off to the canteen for a meal like ravening wolves. We found that the officers who had preceded us were divided into groups or messes, of which we formed the sixth. An energetic subaltern of the Cheshire Regiment, H. C. Randall by name, postponed his own meal in order to cater for our wants. As mess secretary he procured for each of us a plate, a knife, a fork, and a spoon, at the price of one mark for the set. The food was a slice of bread and butter, cheese, and coffee. I think there was also soup.

Our companions in misfortune lost no time in making us welcome and as comfortable as the circumstances permitted. The commandant was a Prussian reservist officer with a long heavy moustache. We were told that he was courteous and considerate in every respect, and that, provided we took care to salute him whenever we passed him, we should find him everything we could reasonably wish.

Supper was at 6 P.M. The same plate did duty for both courses, soup and meat, the more fastidious taking it under the pump in the interval. When the meal was over the junior members of the messes did the washing up. After supper we walked a mile, as the old adage recommends. We soon knew to a nicety how many turns round the court made up this distance, and some active spirits improved on the advice by walking several miles. At 8.30 a bugle sounded, and everyone had to retire to his room; at 9 sounded "lights out." That first night was memorable for the little occupants which we found already in possession of our beds. Just when we hoped we had finished our labours for the day these little bed-fellows began theirs. The more we wanted to sleep, the more wakeful they became. Scratching, tossing, and—it must be owned—a little mild swearing could be heard, where snoring would have been much more tolerable. A diversion occurred at about 10 P.M., when four new-comers arrived in the room. These were Major A. Yate, K.O.Y.L.I., Captain W. Roche and Lieut. J. L. Hardy, Connaught Rangers, and Lieut. E. B. Budden of the Middlesex Regiment (T.F.) They had had hairbreadth escapes, of which we heard only the faintest outline that night. We gave them some chocolate to stave off their hunger—all that we had to offer, except the advice not to sleep in bed, but on the floor. Those who did not take it repented in the morning when they looked at their swollen faces in the glass.

At 6 A.M. reveillé sounded, and before it was finished Major Yate was up and out of bed. I followed his example, and then the two of us began a practice which we kept up while the warm weather lasted, namely, a cold bath under the pump in the solitude of the courtyard. The shower-bath was not open at that early hour, and when it was, the competition made it less attractive than our substitute for the morning tub. Poor Major Yate! He attempted to escape ten days later, and lost his life in so doing. One of the sentries affirmed that he shot him as he made his way through the barbed wire, and that the Major fled wounded into the river, from which he never came forth alive. He was a great loss to us, being a fluent speaker of German. His memory was prodigious; he learnt up the names and addresses of all his fellow-prisoners in order to notify their relatives in case he succeeded in his attempt. He has since been awarded posthumously the Victoria Cross for his gallantry in the campaign.

TORGAU

Our first complete day in the new surroundings was Saturday. There was a general wish for Divine Service on the morrow, and the Commandant signified his consent. We selected as our chapel the passage over the entrance at one end of the building. There was an inspiring atmosphere about that first service. Our altar was a dormitory table, our altar linen a couple of white handkerchiefs, our chalice a twopenny wine-glass (the best we could procure), our paten an ordinary dinner-plate. Pews, of course, there were none, and as for books, we were fortunate enough to have one, a hymn-book, prayer-book, and Bible bound together in a single volume, which I was carrying in my haversack at the time we were captured. The pew difficulty was overcome by each officer bringing his stool. The lack of books made no difference to the heartiness of the service, for the hymns and chants were familiar to most of us from childhood. The mighty volume of sound that went up that morning in hymns of thankfulness and praise was a never-to-be-forgotten sensation to those who heard it or joined in it. The place whereon we stood was holy ground, and it was good for us to be there.

After Matins came the celebration of the Holy Communion, and it was as solemn as the preparatory service had been hearty. It mattered nothing that we had around us none of the appurtenances which decency and order require when they can be had. We were thinking of other things than those.

As the weeks passed and our numbers increased, this pro-cathedral failed to satisfy our needs. One Saturday at the roll-call parade Colonel W. E. Gordon, V.C., our senior officer, announced that the subalterns, who occupied a large shed adjoining the fortress and within its walls, had spontaneously placed their dormitory at the public disposal for Divine Service. This was an improvement on the open landing, since it was quieter, and was large enough to accommodate the whole congregation at a single service. From the first Sunday,

38 IN THE HANDS OF THE ENEMY

it should be added, we held an evening service, which was no less hearty than the morning one.

During the week many officers would borrow the book and copy out hymns for the following Sunday in notebooks, which they called the "Torgau Hymnal," thus enlarging the scope of our selection. There was one hymn which we rarely omitted, and generally said or sang on our knees as a prayer, namely, the familiar 595, "For Absent Friends." It seemed to provide a link between ourselves, our comrades at the front, the old folks at home, and One above:

> "Holy Father, in Thy mercy
> Hear our anxious prayer,
> Keep our loved ones, now far absent,
> 'Neath Thy care.
> . . . .
> When in sorrow, when in danger,
> When in loneliness,
> In Thy love look down and comfort
> Their distress."

The time soon came when we aspired to still higher things. Hitherto we had been quite content to rough it, but within a month after our arrival I was able one Sunday to announce that a loft in one of the out-buildings had been assigned to us for use as a chapel, and added that if members of the congregation who possessed a talent for carpentry would offer their services, we might, with the aid of such tools and materials as we could find, beg, or buy, make it worthy of a House of God. At the close of the service several officers gave in their names to the churchwardens as volunteers. "And what is more," said one of them, a Highlander, "I have got tools on my person now!"

We met accordingly on the following morning to the number of more than a dozen, including Lieut.-Col. R. C. Bond, D.S.O., K.O.Y.L.I., and Major (now Lieut.-Col.) P. H. Collingwood, R.A.M.C., churchwardens; Captains E. E. Pearson, J. A. Campbell, and Lieut. T. L. George, Suffolk Regiment; Lieut. (now Captain) C. H. Rawdon, K.O.Y.L.I.; Lieut. Sir Alfred Hick-

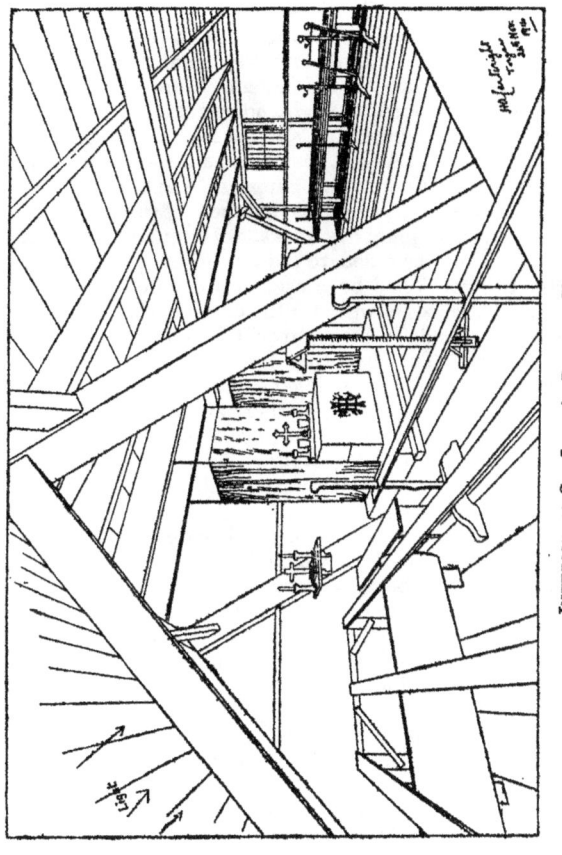

INTERIOR OF ST. LUKE'S CHAPEL, TORGAU

man, Bart., 4th Dragoon Guards; Lieut. (now Captain) W. W. Wagstaff, Bedfordshire Regiment; Lieuts. the Master of Saltoun, H. A. Pelham Burn, and D. W. Hunter Blair, Gordon Highlanders; Lieut. J. Berry, South Lancs. Regiment; Captains A. S. Williams and A. J. Brown, R.A.M.C.; and Lieut. (now Captain) W. G. Barker, Connaught Rangers. Captain Pearson and Lieut. Barker acted as foremen of works. The room had two immense racks, with numerous arms jutting out to accommodate saddles, which showed that before the war it had been used as a mobilisation storeroom. These racks were far too cumbrous either to be allowed to remain in the room or to be removed through the doorway. They had, therefore, to be taken to pieces. When this was done, an ingenious officer saw in them the material for pews. Another officer went out into the passage and saw with one eye two square wooden frameworks and with the other an altar platform of two steps. But the transformation in each case took several days of hard work.

Then as for tools. These consisted of a clumsy old saw of German pattern which broke before the work was finished, a chisel, a plane, a pair of pincers, and a hammer, all of them borrowed from German carpenters engaged in the fort, by a judicious use of *bakshish*. Nails were obtained in a similar manner.

The day on which the work was complete and the dedication made was St. Luke's Day. Consequently it was known thenceforth as St. Luke's Chapel. It was necessary to have a collection to defray the cost. The amount required was announced at the time, and when the churchwardens came to count the money, it came to the exact sum *plus* five pfennigs ($\frac{1}{2}d$.). "What a strange thing!" I remarked. "No, I do not think it is strange," said one of the churchwardens; and he was right.

One morning I was walking round the court with Sir A. Hickman when he made a proposal which introduced a new feature into our services: "Why not form a choir?" In response to an appeal arising out of this

TORGAU 41

suggestion, about twenty-five officers formed themselves into a choir under the leadership of Captain P. C. T. Davy, R.A.M.C. Their names were: Major N. W. Barlow, Hants Regiment, and Major A. C. R. Nutt and Captain J. E. T. Younger, R.F.A.; Captains V. R. Tahourdin, C. A. K. Matterson, and Lieut. W. G. R. Elliot, D.S.O., Cheshire Regiment; Captain Maclean of Ardgour, A. and S. H.; Captain H. S. Jervis, and Lieut. R. D. Mosely, R. Munster Fusiliers; Lieut. W. G. Barker, Conn. Rangers; Lieut. C. H. West, R. Dublin Fusiliers; Lieut. A. E. B. Anderson, R. Irish Regiment; Captain L. Simpson, and Lieuts. H. B. Hibbert and J. B. Noel, K.O.Y.L.I.; Lieut. J. G. Swayne, Somerset L.I.; Lieut. Sir A. Hickman, 4th Dragoon Guards; Lieut. R. G. Peek, 7th Lancers; Lieut. T. L. George, Suffolk Regiment; Lieut. C. G. Graves, R. Scots; Lieuts. J. F. H. Houldsworth, H. L. Pelham Burn, and D. W. Hunter Blair, Gordon Highlanders; Lieut. W. Clark, Irish Rifles; Captain A. J. Brown, R.A.M.C.; and Dr. A. R. Elliot, British Red Cross Society. In spite of having no musical setting to hymns or chants, their rendering of the service with alto, tenor, and bass parts was wonderfully accurate. When we were able to obtain a harmonium the Hon. Rupert Keppel, Coldstream Guards, presided at it, playing from memory and ear, with the innate feeling of a true musician. Lance-Corporal Higgins, Gordon Highlanders, acted as church orderly.

As time went on, our numbers increased to about 230 British officers, and 800 French officers joined us from Maubeuge, including four generals. One of the latter had been interned in Torgau before, in the 1870 war, and had made good his escape. The authorities guarded against the recurrence of such an eventua'ity on the present occasion, their most elaborate precaution being the enlistment of dogs to reinforce the sentries. Their barkings could be heard occasionally by night, but their presence disturbed neither our repose nor our equanimity. The following effusion gained currency

42 IN THE HANDS OF THE ENEMY

amongst us. I cannot remember its origin, but in the absence of testimony to the contrary, we will credit it to the wit of a British officer :

AUFRUF (APPEAL)
Extract from the *Torgau Kriegsblatt*.

"Already hundreds of thousands of prisoners of war are now in Germany. It is expected that there will be hordes more coming. Large numbers of troops have to be called out to act as guards, and heavy claims are made on their powers of endurance and resource. Moreover, as the experience of the years 1870–1 teaches, the guards are exposed to malicious and sudden attacks. This danger is greater than at that time on account of the bitter hatred and spiteful temper of our enemy.

"Our brave guards will certainly not shrink from the strain, and will courageously face the dangers. We can, however, lighten their task considerably and reduce the dangers to a minimum by furnishing them with dogs to accompany and defend them. The following breeds serve best as watch-dogs : sheep dogs, Yorkshire terriers (of these two breeds those that are not required as hospital dogs), Airedale terriers, deerhounds. Great Danes, bull dogs, and other hounds. They must be strong, powerful animals at least a year old. Dogs older than two years are not suitable, as they are usually difficult to train.

"All owners of suitable dogs in the district of Torgau, &c., are therefore requested to notify the Garrison Commandant at Torgau, and to send in writing exact particulars of their dogs (breed, age, and whether already trained). As this is for a patriotic object, it is asked that dogs be supplied free of charge. As soon as they are no longer required they will be restored to their owners. By reason of their activity, it is practically out of the question that the dogs will come to any harm. In case, however, a dog should die (as is always possible), the owner will be compensated."

TORGAU

Pay was issued to us at the rate of 100 marks a month for captains and upwards, 60 marks for subalterns. We paid for our meals, which worked out at about 1½ marks a day. After the first week or two the messing arrangements were handed over to a French

A GERMAN GUARD AND HIS GUARDIAN

officer, who carried out his difficult task efficiently. The meals, though far from sumptuous and not always palatable, were sufficient for our needs. There were few of the amenities to which officers are accustomed in a mess at home, such as table-cloths and cleanliness. When orderlies were brought in to do the washing up and fetch the dishes from the kitchen we were relieved of those duties. The large influx of officers necessitated the building of sheds in a large compound at the back of the fortress, which was then placed at our disposal for exercise ground. The passages in the semi-circular building, upstairs and downstairs, were allocated to the British officers for their meals, and were accordingly fitted up with tables. The French officers took their meals in a large shed in the compound erected for the purpose.

During the last two months of our stay at Torgau I occupied a small room in the centre of the building with Major (now Lieut.-Col.) A. G. Thompson, Major W. H. Long, and Captain P. C. T. Davy, of the R.A.M.C., as companions. Like the Hindus, we divided ourselves into exclusive castes, as far as the necessary duties in connexion with the room were concerned. The Colonel (as we may call him by anticipation) lit the stove, the Major washed the cups and saucers, the Captain swept the floor, and I, with the assistance of a member of our mess, brought in the coal. We resented interference, however well meant, by any of the other three outside his proper caste, for we invariably found that in such cases the work was not properly done. At first, regarding it as undignified for the Colonel to be allowed to engage in so menial a task as lighting the stove, we endeavoured to relieve him of it. But the good-natured officer found fault so emphatically, not to say eloquently, with the amateurish manner in which the work was done unless he had done it himself, that we decided ever afterwards to allow him a free hand. Stringent rules regulated the drawing of coal. At 2 P.M. daily a long procession of officers and orderlies formed up outside the coalhouse, in pairs, armed with a double-handed tin box awaiting the arrival of "Mossy-face," the barrack warden. He might be punctual or he might not, but it was risky to count upon his unpunctuality, because your place in the procession would be lost. Lieut. Clark ticked off on a list the representatives of each mess as he passed in, and Mossy-face kept a sharp eye open lest anyone should attempt to carry off more than his proper ration.

Mossy-face's duties included the superintendence of the shower-bath. He was heard to remark that if officers were so insistent upon having baths, there would be few survivors once the cold weather set in. When we first arrived he had adopted the rôle of a gaoler in his demeanour towards us, but after a while he became civil and deferential, and—when his son was captured in the war—actually sympathetic.

In the main building was a canteen where we used to jostle one another to obtain our purchases, so inadequate was it in size. It was dirty, ill-ventilated, and badly conducted, and the attendants behind the counter lacked civility. Here were obtainable underclothing, toilet requisites, as well as tobacco, apples, sausages, white rolls, cake, and coffee. For a while beer was to be obtained, but latterly this and the white rolls were forbidden. In the larger compound was a small canteen in the shape of a wooden booth. We have happier recollections of this one, for the civilian in charge of it, and his wife, were far more amenable. They obtained not a few little luxuries for us from the town, and behaved towards us with all deference and respect. Madame "Morgen," we used to call the steward's wife, because when we asked for an article not usually on sale, the invariable reply was "Morgen," meaning that we should have it on the following day. Tradespeople from the town attended on certain days, such as booksellers, opticians, tailors, and bootmakers. Those who wished to purchase trousers were supplied with brown corduroys, a red stripe adorning the outer seam in order to give them a military appearance and to make escape more difficult, though a penknife would have removed it in less than a minute.

Both before the orderlies arrived and afterwards we took our turns in potato-peeling at 7 A.M. in the small court. This was less popular than apple-peeling, because young officers felt themselves entitled to a few apples as their perquisite when engaged in the latter occupation.

Every morning about two hundred women used to come in under escort to engage in the work of packing shells in a shed at the north-east corner of the larger court. They were marched away at night and their places taken by other women. The finished article was continually being carried out in wagons and sent away.

It was a subject of universal regret when the first Commandant resigned his position. He was succeeded by an officer of less gentlemanly instincts, who conceived a bad impression of us at the outset of his period of office owing to an unfortunate incident. He was holding a roll-call of the French officers in the large court whilst a football match was being played by some of our people. Unfortunately the ball was accidentally or through some boyish freak passed through the Frenchmen's lines. The Commandant had some difficulty in finding words to express his indignation. He appealed to us, in a letter to the senior British officer, to live up to the tradition of " Germanic-Anglo-Saxon politeness." Colonel Gordon apologised officially, and we all regretted the incident. Nothing was farther from our thoughts than to behave in the manner in which our conduct was interpreted.

During his first few days the Commandant had some notice or other posted up to emphasise the necessity of our living up to the tradition above quoted. The following is a translation of one of them:

> "Every day applications from British officers reach me which are so entirely without justification that it is not worth my while to take any notice of them. Officers appear still not to realise the fact that, as prisoners of war, they have not so much rights as duties. They are not to take up my time with the expression of foolish wishes.
>
> " If this state of things, which betrays a certain bumptiousness on the part of British officers, does not cease, I shall take the opportunity to put into each room a French sub-lieutenant risen from the

ranks, and I shall further apply that a proportion of your allies the Russian officers may share your rooms.

"This order of mine is to be posted up in the British quarters. Will you please, Colonel, report to me in German, the fact that these instructions have been obeyed?

"(Sgd.) BRAUN, Captain,
"Officer, i/c Prisoners' Depôt."

What the applications complained of were I do not know, but they are not likely to have been unreasonable, because nothing was submitted to the Commandant except through the senior officer, who was very particular as to everything he passed on. Possibly the reference may have been to an application which was made by the medical officers and myself to be returned to the seat of war in accordance with the provisions of the Geneva Convention.

On the other hand, this Commandant was responsible for the best arrangement with respect to a roll-call that we met with in our experiences. This arrangement was that we should parade daily at 10.30 A.M. as follows:

(a) R.F.A. and "mounted" troops under Lieut.-Col. C. F. Stevens, C.M.G., R.F.A.

(b) Staff and infantry under Lieut.-Col. C. M. Stephenson, K.O.S.B.

(c) Departmental officers and others not included in the above, under Major A. G. Thompson, R.A.M.C.

The whole were to parade in two ranks, with an interval of one pace between the parties, under the senior officer, who at first was Colonel W. E. Gordon, V.C., A.D.C. Each party was to fall in by seniority of regiments. "Officers and others on parade," so the order ran, "must be properly dressed, pipes not visible. Officers in charge of parties will *minutely* inspect the dress of their parties, and report absentees to the Commandant through the senior British officer." When Colonel S. C. F. Jackson, D.S.O., Hampshire Regiment, arrived, the command of this parade passed to him. Both he and his predecessor were ably assisted in their duties by Major G. H. F. Tailyour, R.F.A.

The same Commandant subsequently laid us under another obligation, though quite unintentionally. He asked us whether we would care to subscribe to the German Red Cross Society. Now this was a Society of which many of our number had, I regret to say, far from pleasant experiences, and was the last they would care to support. Colonel Gordon, at that time our senior, with the kindly Christian feeling which was characteristic of him, regarded this as an opportunity for displaying a large mind and for returning good for evil. He therefore strongly commended the suggestion. Some cordially agreed with him; others as cordially disapproved. Eventually it occurred to a brilliant genius that if subscriptions were paid by cheques, through a neutral bank, our relatives at home would be put out of suspense by at least hearing that we were alive. Objections vanished like the mist before the sun. Cheques were made out on odd bits of paper. A sum amounting to over £80 passed to the credit of the Society, and the news was in this manner spread in England that we were still in the land of the living.

The effect of some of those cheques in English homes was to turn many a house of mourning into a house of rejoicing. For the names which appeared on many of them had already figured on the roll of killed in the English newspapers, together with an obituary paragraph. In fact one day an officer went up to a table where four of his friends were playing bridge, and laid before them a cutting from a newspaper which recorded the death of three of them. "This is the first time," remarked one of them, Colonel Bond, to his partner, "that you have played bridge with three dead men." The partner was Major A. E. Haig, K.O.S.B., who, as we shall see in a later chapter, was himself a "dead man."

We are, however, anticipating the time when letters first began to arrive. Tuesday, October 6, was a red-letter day. Colonel Gordon announced that we were to be allowed to send postcards home! The heaviest hearts were now like feathers. Who that saw it, or formed part of it, will ever forget the long queue which drew up in the southern archway, where Major Gray, our postmaster, sat selling postcards at five pfennigs apiece? Each dropped his coin into a jam-pot as he received a card. A few hours later we returned to deposit them, the bearers of many a loving, tender message, in a haversack which did duty as a pillar-box outside Colonel Gordon's door. The postcards were double, one half being for the reply. Our own half was ruled with six lines, and began with the printed words, "I am in good health, prisoner of war." . . . The reply half had also six lines, and began with, "Family in good health at," . . . and closed, in brackets, with the words, "(No news of military operations)."

October 10 was another red-letter day. For then we received the first letters from home. This for many of us was the first time we had had any communication with those most near and dear to us since we bade them farewell, nearly three months before.

All this put us into the best of humours. Not that there was ever very much depression. If anyone was downcast, as a rule he nursed his feelings in his own bosom. Indeed, the brave and cheery manner in which the early and most trying days of our captivity were borne was truly wonderful. Humour was extracted from the least pleasant experiences. "Keep smiling" seemed to be the general motto. Regulations and indignities which might have been calculated to annoy and dishearten were submitted to without a word and often with amusement. The British spirit is not easily perturbed. Major B. Chetwynd-Stapylton, Cheshire Regiment, deserves special mention in this connexion, and won for himself the title of "The Optimist." He was wont to say that if anyone appeared to be a pessimist, he was not actually so, but merely expressed gloomy views in order to hear them answered.

50 IN THE HANDS OF THE ENEMY

The delightful companionship caused the days to pass not too slowly, and when we were able to obtain books, the time simply sped along. What with literature indoors and games out of doors (which a later chapter will describe), everyone maintained the *mens sana in corpore sano*. During these months, it should be added, one or two officers were still suffering from wounds, and received skilful attention at the hands of our own medical officers.

The twenty orderlies, whose arrival made such a difference to our comfort, lived in a shed in the large court under the superintendence of Sergt. Tyte, 9th Lancers. In leisure hours they took their turn on the football field. A friendly spirit was evinced between their officers and them. They kept their end up well, as they would themselves express it. A few of them picked up a smattering of French, and one of them taught himself German.

We often dreamt and spoke of the day when we should march out of Torgau. There were two destinations only which came within the range of our contemplation—one was Berlin, and the other was England. Meanwhile, however, there was a place of four short letters which was to be our home for six long months.

VI.—THE JOURNEY TO BURG

On Tuesday, November 24, the rumour was noised about that a turning in the lane was about to come on the morrow, that, in fact, the British prisoners were to be removed to Burg, near Magdeburg. Now rumours soon circulated. Half an hour was less than was needed to inform the whole *Lager* of anything that might be in the wind. These rumours were the daily topic of conversation, and as they were always fresh, and nearly always imaginative, our life was kept at a pitch of excitement. Some cheery members of our party made it their business to have a new rumour pass from

A German Sentry doing his Bit

THE JOURNEY TO BURG

lip to lip at least once a week, and calculated how long it took to get it back from their lips to their ears—never more than two hours. We always inquired where a rumour came from, and credited or discredited it accordingly. The best rumours were those which originated from the German priest. He would mention some news to the French chaplain on one of the latter's visits to the town, who told the senior French general, who told his orderly, who passed it on to his English companion, who circulated it everywhere—and there was the tale that rumour built.

The rumour in question had the highest of all origins. It came from the Commandant himself. There could be no reason or room for doubt. It did not please us, for we had adapted ourselves to the circumstances, and felt that any change would be one for the worse. We liked our quarters, although overcrowded; we now had a Commandant who was at any rate humane; and some of us had made friends of the Allies. It would take a considerable time to get a new set of conditions, in a state of captivity, to compare with these. Consequently we walked about the courts with sad faces. It was a fine chance for optimists and pessimists to air their respective views. "It is certain to be a change for the better," said the one. "It will be out of the frying-pan into the fire," replied the other. Those who belonged definitely to neither of these groups suspended their opinion.

The saddest aspect of the proposed move to a large number was the dismantling of our chapel which it would involve: "The handsomest little sanctuary I have ever seen," a young officer described it on the day when it had to be taken to pieces. Captain H. A. Cartwright, Middlesex Regiment, drew a sketch of it, spending the whole afternoon at the task, although his fingers were almost too cold to hold a pencil. (*Vide* p. 39.)

A larger congregation than usual attended the daily Evensong that evening at 5, after which they all remained behind to lend a hand in the task of

52 IN THE HANDS OF THE ENEMY

demolition. The work of a week was undone in a quarter of an hour. The altar hangings and sacred vessels were packed up to carry with us. Lieut. C. M. Usher, Gordon Highlanders, the international footballer, carried away the Bible—the International Book —to pack it amongst his kit. Lieut. G. W. R. Elliot, D.S.O., Cheshire Regiment, carried off the lamps. Whatever we could not take away we presented to the French chapel. And then, like the Israelites of old, we went sorrowfully away, leaving our sanctuary not a "heap of stones," but a dilapidated heap of timber. At the same time we carried off happy memories which no rumours, true or false, could touch with unholy hands as long as we lived.

The following morning 150 of us were ordered to be prepared to quit Torgau at midday. The names were read out at roll-call, and we were divided into two groups according to our fate. Those who were "for it," on the right; those who were not, on the left. I found myself in the latter group. Luggage was to be deposited in the small court by 11.45—in the snow. It was a strange pile. All shapes and sizes of parcels and boxes lay there ready to be carted off. Personal luggage, and such treasures as could not be entrusted to German transport had to be worn upon the back, or carried in the hand.

The party fell in at 12.30, and at 1 marched off to the station. Most of the French, and all the British officers, assembled in the court to wave them a silent farewell. All cheering was *verboten*. Snow was falling on the picturesque procession as it passed out of the gates with Colonel Jackson at its head.

The early part of the next morning was spent by those of us who were left behind in bidding farewell to French friends, and in packing up our kit for the journey. Happy were those who had fewest possessions to stow away. One or two were the proud owners of sleeping valises, into which they were able to cram all their belongings with ease. Some used a sack for this

THE JOURNEY TO BURG 53

purpose; others bought suit-cases and knapsacks from the canteen. As for me, I put all my worldly goods into the soldier's pack which I found at Landrecies, and strapped it on my back. Note-books, letters, and papers were carried in a saddle wallet in the hand; and a few odds and ends went into a haversack.

At 11.30 a rough-and-ready meal was served, without any of the customary utensils, such as plates, knives, forks, and spoons. No one was over particular about his table manners in the circumstances. We had the appetite of savages, and adopted their habits in the way we disposed of our food.

The proceedings of the previous day on the square were repeated. The French attended in full strength to give us a hearty shake of the hand. We stood in two ranks—about eighty in all—for quite half an hour, laden with as much luggage as we dared venture to "stagger under" (as one of our number expressed it), whilst the authorities counted us over two or three times to make certain that no one lurked behind. It must have been a comical sight—a strange assortment of officers of various regiments and corps, some attired in greatcoats, of German and English patterns, others in Burberrys; some in Balaclava helmets, and a few without headgear of any kind; all bulging out in front, behind, and at the sides. One officer had a long loaf of brown bread sticking out of his coat pocket. In front of me stood a short medical officer, and beside him stood a herculean colonel at least a foot taller. The usual command to "stand at ease," though given out, could not be obeyed to the letter, because few hands were free to be clasped behind the back, which that command involves.

Whilst we were in this constrained posture the German guard drew up in front and to rear of us, loaded rifles, and fixed bayonets. The cart conveying our heavy baggage, such as mess kit, then drove off. "Left turn! Quick march!" Away we went through the great heavy gates which had shut us in for exactly three months. The lingering look behind was not untouched with sadness. We had made ourselves happy in the circumstances, and the associations contained the memory of friendships formed and quiet hours spent such as we might not so easily obtain elsewhere in Germany. We would far rather " bear those ills we had than fly to others that we knew not of."

At the same time, the clang of the closing doors was like the striking of another hour in the long day of captivity. Moreover, it was something to see the outside of those thick walls, and to look over the side of the splendid bridge which spans the Elbe. " Tramp, tramp, tramp," resounded its planks under our feet. Our packs were heavy, but our hearts were light.

The route lay past the Hartenfels Schloss with its memories of Luther, and with its foundation and restoration dates—1534 and 1801—marked on its stone walls. We gathered a dense and denser crowd, like a snowball gathering snow, as we rolled onward to the station. The hangers-on were by no means silent, but they were much less insulting than when we had travelled along the same road in the opposite direction three months before. Not that they had abated one jot of their unreasoning hatred of the British nation; but they seemed to have acquired a juster estimate of the British *Schweinhund* (as they were wont to call us), and the town was considerably the richer for our short stay within its walls.

So ended one chapter in our experience as prisoners of war. Though we had not been on active service for our country during that period, perhaps we had learnt to appreciate more highly the fact that we had been born under the Union Jack, and that we were, as such, men with a mission to the world. That this particular part of the world stood in need of such a mission, the sequel will show.

Arrived at the station, we were bundled into third-class carriages, with such of our baggage as we could find room for. In one such carriage five of us made ourselves as comfortable as we could. Three German

THE JOURNEY TO BURG 55

privates—our guard—deposited themselves in three corner seats, with loaded rifles in their hands. Their charge consisted of three medical officers, a wounded officer, and a chaplain. Each compartment was similarly guarded. Their first proceeding was to close the windows. I protested that we had two doctors present who would certainly insist on having fresh air for the benefit of our health, with the result that one window was opened half an inch for about five minutes, and then it was closed. Two or three times during the journey we got it open again.

The soldier sitting next to me had been brought up at the Manchester Grammar School, and was now a master of languages at a German school. He was friendly and communicative, but not at first. I asked him whither we were bound. "Couldn't say." So *I* told *him* we were off to Burg. When he found we knew so much he became less cautious in his remarks.

The four officers whiled away the first part of the journey with a game of bridge, and our guard looked on, smoking cigars which they took from inside their caps, keeping their rifles handy all the time in case of "odd tricks." No "grand slam" occurred, and we reached Wittenberg still on the inside of the compartment's doors. At 4 P.M. we felt that we would like a meal, so we took down a long loaf of brown bread and a box of sardines, of which we gave our German friends a share. Soon afterwards they produced from their pockets a newspaper parcel each, containing a thick sandwich of bread and cheese. They did not offer to share this meal with us, nor did they dare to ask the impartial Red Cross "ministering angels" (as some of our officers called them) to give us a cup of cocoa, when these were being handed in at the window at one or two stations on the journey. They were of an appetising nature, it appeared, for each soldier found it quite easy to put away three mugs of it before his thirst was satisfied.

At Wittenberg my thoughts went back to Luther and his association with this town. He too knew what it

56 IN THE HANDS OF THE ENEMY

was to be a prisoner, although not a *Kriegsgefangene*. This proved cold comfort, however, as cold almost as the cup of coffee which, by the kind offices of one of our German companions, was smuggled in in a beer bottle handed out by us for the purpose. Had he asked for it openly for us he would have brought jeers upon himself from his own people.

By this time it was dusk, and the incandescent lamp in the carriage was not in working order. We feared we might have to pass the remaining half of the journey in the dark, and our guard seeming to entertain the same fear asked the station officials for a night-light. Had they visions of our giving them the slip in the dark, or, worse still, of giving them their *quietus* with the butt end of their own rifles ? Or, was their action purely unselfish ? We gave them the benefit of the doubt, and enjoyed to the full the dim light placed in the circular globe above our heads.

The next stop was at Magdeburg, where we remained with blinds drawn for half an hour. We were none the less aware that we were objects of interest to those who caught a glimpse of us.

Everything that we had as yet experienced was tame as compared with what was in store for us when we reached Burg at about 9·30 P.M. Our arrival was evidently expected by a mob, who were bent on enjoying themselves at our expense. We were hustled out, bag and baggage, on to the platform, with more haste than ceremony. Hardly was time given us to get into fours. The crowd broke into " *Deutschland, Deutschland über Alles,*" in Haydn's beautiful tune, which the Austrians use as the setting to their National Anthem, and which we use as the accompaniment to " Praise the Lord, ye heavens adore Him."

We provided much entertainment to the crowd, who escorted us alongside of the guard, the latter's bayonets fixed as before. One burly doctor (Major W. H. Long) marched partly like a Swahili, with his heavy valise balanced on his head ; partly like a pack-mule, with

THE JOURNEY TO BURG

his medical panniers hanging on each side. Another doctor (Captain Stevenson, R.A.M.C.) carried his luggage Kikuyu-wise on his neck and back, and its weight could not have been less than 50 lbs., but a cheery Irish voice betrayed his real nationality.

Some officers carried in their hands loads which were heavy enough almost to pull their arms out of their sockets, so heavy, in fact, that one or two were compelled to drop them and leave them where they fell. There was no stopping to recover these unless at the risk of a coarse "Hurry up" in German, or, in one or two exceptional cases, a prod from a rifle in the back. One officer, at least, and he a colonel, was subjected to this indignity. Remarks, jests, and jeers were thrown freely at us, but we were either too heavily laden to pay attention to them, or too ignorant of the language in which they were spoken to understand them. One never realised before how appropriate is the old Roman term for baggage—*impedimenta*; nor how true is the French proverb, "*Peu de biens, peu de soin.*"

On reaching our prison-house the order went forth, "Irish Roman Catholic officers to the front!" We learnt afterwards the meaning of this mysterious command. The counting process was next gone through, not an easy matter since we were in no sort of regular formation by this time. Having satisfied themselves that no "convicts" had escaped, we filed into the sleeping rooms. The one into which I was marched was typical of the rest. A long, low dormitory with wooden roof resting on iron girders, supported by three iron pillars down the centre of the room; the walls partly of brick and partly of wood. Eight beds were arranged along the wall opposite the door, nine along the wall facing these, and eight between the pillars in the centre, twenty-five in all.

Nine strange heads and bearded faces popped up from as many cots as we entered the room, and greetings in a tongue, also strange, offered us what was obviously a welcome. These proved to be our Russian allies. Dropping our loads on vacant cots we at once entered into conversation with these sharers of our lot, in French, a language which some of them spoke quite fluently. There were about 200 Russian officers in the *Lager*, they told us, and about 50 French; this chamber was our dining-room as well as our bedroom; our food was provided by the Germans at 48 marks a month, which was deducted from our pay; the lights (electric) were allowed to remain on until ten; no reveillé in the morning.

Whilst we acquired this information a Russian orderly brought in a bowl of sausages, a slice of brown bread, and a cup of tea for each of us. Two blankets, brand new, one single sheet, and a double sheet (sewn down the sides in the form of what is known in the Army as a "flea-bag") lay on each bed, and we proceeded to arrange them according to our different tastes. To unpack and undress was the work of a few minutes, and soon we had tucked ourselves in with the half light-hearted, half home-sick feelings of schoolboys returning after the holidays. Relief at the conclusion of an unpleasant experience helped to dim for the time the memory of it, and sleep soon blotted it out completely.

VII.—BURG: SETTLING IN

It has been mentioned that on the night of our arrival members of Irish regiments were specially called aside. We learnt on the morrow that they were to have a larger, airier, and more comfortable room, apart from their former companions and from the Allies. This was intended to be but the beginning of special privileges with a view to undermining their loyalty. One by one they were interviewed in private, and asked certain questions, such as, Would they care to serve in the German army against England? and, Was it a fact that the Munster Fusiliers had fired upon the King's Own Scottish

BURG: SETTLING IN

Borderers in revenge for Major A. E. Haig's order to that regiment to fire on the citizens of Dublin in the riots before the war? The purpose of the inquiry evidently was to find out whether the loyalty of Irish-

OUR RUSSIAN FRIENDS GROW BEARDS, BUT AT DIFFERENT ELEVATIONS

men was a weak point in the British armour. Until we reached Burg and brought "the notorious Major Haig" with us the newspaper report was believed which stated that in the alleged reprisals upon the K.O.S.B. Major Haig had been shot. That officer was the object of special curiosity, and one of the German officials asked in my hearing whether it was really the

60 IN THE HANDS OF THE ENEMY

case that he was there in the flesh! It opened their eyes to find that the Major was not only alive, but no less popular with the Irish than with the other officers.

We now had opportunities of making the acquaintance of our Russian allies at close quarters. First impressions were decidedly favourable. They appeared for the most part to be fine handsome men. The Russian uniform in colour is not unlike our own, a green shade of khaki, worn by some officers loose, like a smock, with a leather belt round the waist; by others a closer-fitting serge was worn. The trousers and riding-breeches are of the same shade, with a thin red stripe down the outer seam; the boots are of the Wellington type; the cap has a peak and badge in front.

Although we were allies against a common foe, and as time went on became close friends, it must be acknowledged that on one point we were at first obliged to join issue with them. To have the window open by day or by night in the winter-time was to them as one of the deadly sins, whereas to us it was the very breath of life. So much was this the case with us that one of the first things we had done on the previous evening was to go straight to the windows on our side of the room and open one of them. This had the effect of bringing a Russian officer out of his bed to protest. He closed the window in the politest manner possible, gesticulating with his hands because the language difficulty made it impossible for him to explain by word of mouth. Captain W. L. Dugmore, Cheshire Regiment, whose bed was next to the window, made gesticulations likewise to the effect that the opposite side of the room was the Russian quarter, and this the British. Again our friend moved his hand rapidly to and fro in front of his body. Like the German lady who "understood, but didn't mean to," the offending officer seized it in a friendly fashion, shook it kindly but firmly, and bowed. The Russian also bowed, returned to his bed, and the Englishman re-opened the window. A peaceful settlement was thus happily arrived at, and thenceforward as long as we occupied that room the window remained open for the greater part of the day and the whole of the night. In another room at a later period a similar difficulty arose, but was promptly settled by Col. C. F. Stevens, R.F.A., who, with an irresistible combination of tact and firmness, removed one of the windows bodily from its hinges and placed it under his bed!

The Russians, we were told, had been warned by the Germans before our arrival that we were peculiar as a race on the subject of fresh air. Some went so far as to say that it was expected, and even hoped, that we might quarrel, and suggested that this was the reason for our being herded together, instead of being given separate rooms. If this was really so we disappointed them, for the relations between the Allies and ourselves continued to be cordial and friendly to the end.

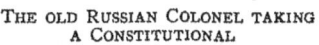
THE OLD RUSSIAN COLONEL TAKING A CONSTITUTIONAL

Any trivial differences such as the incidents above alluded to provided more amusement than annoyance. There was invariably a readiness on both sides to give and take.

The Russians had with them a small boy, about twelve years old, whom we called "the powder monkey." We were informed that the Russian army employed such to carry ammunition to the firing line. The brave little fellow was as much a curiosity to us as Trumpeter Berry had proved to the French peasants along the line of march.

Let us make a tour of inspection round our new home. It was roughly oblong in shape. In peace time it appeared to have been used for the storage of wagons and mobilisation equipment. There was a double row of two-storeyed sheds parallel to each other, and a similar shed beyond them on the right-hand side, making five in all. Some of the sheds had obviously been used as stables, others for storing wagons. A wall formed the boundary at the far end, and a wall, from which the entrance gates opened, at the other end; both were of wood, surmounted by a palisade of barbed wire. The space enclosed between the walls and sheds—about 160 yards by 30—supplied our exercise ground, where we walked up and down, down and up, to our hearts' content, at first picking our steps, for at the time of our arrival it was little more than a morass. Our numbers at that time were over 300, and they afterwards rose to 500, so we took consolation from the thought that when we went out for a walk we got a touch of Piccadilly. Nor was this the only touch. We also had our "clubs." There were two diminutive canteens, which for a time went by the names of the "Ritz" and the "Carlton." The smaller one was divided into two rooms, serving respectively as a shop and a restaurant. The larger one comprised a single room, with the cooking apparatus at one side, and a number of small tables, such as are seen in an A.B.C. shop, on the other. At both of them all the cooking was done in the rooms, and the only ventilation was that which was provided by the opening and closing of the door as customers entered and left.

What the public-house is to the working man, these two canteens soon became to us. They were the popular places of rendezvous for a meal and a chat. Here we used to treat one another to a white roll or a cake, and a cup of excellent coffee; and, until they were put on the *verboten* list, to a chop or steak. The serving was done under the direction of a kind, motherly *Frau* at the one canteen, and by a polite German boy-waiter at the other. The latter had learnt his art at the Savoy Hotel, and said that he looked forward to returning thither after the war. Both places were a vast improvement on the Torgau régime, where in the restaurant department cleanliness and civility were unknown, and an appetising article of diet rare. And so it came about that when we tired of the stuffy dormitory or the crowded footpath there was solace to be found in the still more crowded and stuffy canteen. This place of refuge, however, soon threatened to become a snare, for our pay was as scanty as the daily ration, and canteen luxuries were expensive. The officials came to the rescue, whatever their motive may have been, by reducing the purchasable articles to a minimum, and then we had to content ourselves with the authorised fare.

The regular meals seemed to be provided by the proprietor of the larger canteen under contract with the German Government. They were served at 8 A.M., 12 noon, and 6.30 P.M. In quality they were superior to the Torgau fare, but in quantity scarcely sufficient in the depth of winter for hungry young men. Still it must be remembered that they cost only 1s. 6d. a day.

Our first experience of dinner was decidedly slow. The opening course was soup served in tea-cups, with *Kriegsbrote*—bread made of rye meal and potato. After an interval of about three-quarters of an hour came pork cutlets. The waiting time was filled up with a cigarette or a pipe by the more placid natures; the impatient walked up and down the room, their faces showing the kind of feelings which surged within. Supper was more punctual, and was thoroughly in keeping with the day, which was Friday. It consisted of uncooked fish, a rare delicacy in that part of the world. In the little mess of five to which I belonged we had for it the best of all sauces, a hungry appetite, and whereas one of us could not touch his portion another ate it for him. The other members of the mess were Major W. H. Long, R.A.M.C.; Captain F. Bell, Gordon Highlanders; Captain L. F. Hepworth, Suffolk Regiment; and Lieut. R. E. G. Phillips, R. Irish Regiment. The food, however, good or bad, mattered little as soon as parcels began to come, which was within a few days of our arrival at Burg. The tinned meat, chocolate, soup, tea, coffee, and cocoa which generous friends at home sent out regularly and in abundance made us independent altogether of the fare provided.

The following is a copy of some of the Standing Orders which we found posted on each door:

" 1. Every sentry has orders to fire on any prisoner attempting to escape, without challenging him.

" 4. No prisoner is allowed to have money or weapons upon him. In the first place [meaning the money], it is to be given to the officer commanding the garrison, with a paper on which is to be written the name of the owner, &c.

" 5. Money sent to prisoners will be taken over by the paymaster, when prisoners will be credited with the money.

" 7. Conversation with civilians, such as barbers, tailors, &c., is strictly forbidden.

" 8. Complaints to be made in writing to the officer commanding the garrison. Prisoners are warned against making ungrounded complaints. Ungrounded complaints, if they are repeated, or complaints which are unjustifiable or against better judgment, will be punished.

" 17. Twice daily at uncertain hours the N.C.O. in charge of rooms is to have a short roll-call, in which he will see that all prisoners are present, and give out any orders.

" 18. Food which is extra to the bill of fare is only allowed with the permission of the doctor.

" 19. Every prisoner must take a shower-bath once a week in the room provided, under the supervision of a N.C.O. The use of the bath is regulated by the officer commanding the garrison."

At the Sunday services — Anglican, Roman, and Russian Orthodox—a German censor was in attendance, in case, as someone suggested, he should hear the Kaiser denounced with "bell, book, and candle." The chapel was an unused dormitory-shed containing two long rows of empty beds, whose snowy white sheets must not be used as pews. Later on the beds were removed.

French and Russian officers were in the habit of standing throughout their services. Our own congregation brought chairs with them, or leant against the back of the cots. The choir took up their position in two rows to left of the extemporised altar. The Anglican services, which were at 9 A.M. and 5 P.M., attracted many Russian officers, including their priest. The hymn, "Lead, kindly Light," seemed particularly to impress the saintly man. Noticing that he was overheard humming it to himself on the way out, he smiled and said, "*Bon!*" On that first Sunday the collection was for the British and Foreign Bible Society, whose promise—afterwards fulfilled—to send us a number of Bibles laid us under an obligation for which we felt deeply grateful. As yet we had but one Bible and no hymn-books with tunes or psalters. The previous day, however, this deficiency was partly made good by the arrival of a parcel containing a few copies of each from the Chaplain-General. As these did not suffice to go round, lots were drawn for them, and great was the disappointment of the unsuccessful. Another parcel, from Prebendary W. S. Swayne, Rector of St. Peter's, Cranley Gardens, contained a Cathedral Psalter with tunes, some very fine altar linen, and clerical robes. They arrived in time to be used at the last service which the Prebendary's son, Lieut. J. G. Swayne, Somerset L.I., a valued member of the choir, was destined to attend with us. Before the next Sunday, much to our regret, he had been transferred to another camp.

A French service preceded our own, and was conducted by the French priest, a middle-aged man, who, though a civilian, was made prisoner because, when he

66 IN THE HANDS OF THE ENEMY

fell into German hands, letters belonging to French soldiers were found in his pockets, which with his characteristic desire to do a good turn he had undertaken to post. For hours daily he was a familiar figure in the court, with his smoking-cap, lay collar, and black tie, walking up and down with a French or British companion.

On that first Sunday many of our officers attended the Russian service in addition to their own, out of interest to see the "use" of the Orthodox Church. The priest was a short, stout man, with long black hair, a short beard, and an extremely kind face. He wore a smart grey cassock under a shabby great-coat, which did not completely cover it, and a black " wide-awake " hat. His benevolent bearing commended him to everyone. The service he conducted is worthy of being described in detail. Standing in front of the dormitory table, which had already served as a Roman and an Anglican altar, he reverently laid upon it a linen cloth, two brass candlesticks, and a heavy brass crucifix. He then lit the candles, leaving the crucifix, which had no pedestal, face uppermost. He wore no other vestment than his grey cassock and black overcoat, but he drew from a paper parcel a green stole, kissed the cross which adorned the back of it, and put it over his shoulders, making at the same time the sign of the cross. This stole was long enough to reach to the foot of his cassock, but resembled the regalia of a Good Templar rather than the pattern usual in the Anglican Communion. It was not uniform in width, but was circular in the upper portion which went round the neck, square in the lower, the two side pieces being fastened with hook and eye from the breast downwards.

The congregation stood behind him, a few paces distant, in three sides of a square, the choir being on his left hand. As they took their places each worshipper crossed himself three times, from left to right; indeed the sign of the cross was made repeatedly throughout the service, apparently whenever any member of the congregation felt moved to do so, on each occasion signing himself thrice. The priest did it less often and more slowly. A spirit of deep devotion pervaded the assembly, and the demeanour of everyone was

A Captive Russian Priest

most reverent. The service seemed to consist of versicles and responses, said by priest and sung by people standing. The choir led the singing divinely. No organ or musical instrument is ever used in the Orthodox Church. Their unaccompanied choirs are said to be beyond all comparison the finest in the world. On the present occasion the compass of the voices, the trueness of the ear, the delicate sensitiveness of feeling enabled the Russian officers to produce effects which thrilled the listener to the depths of his being. Their crescendoes were superb. One minute you heard the deep roll of thunder; the next minute the dying away of a dim, distant echo.

Twice the priest turned and faced the congregation and read a passage from a book, possibly a portion of Scripture. Two or three times during the service all knelt down. The address was not lost even upon those of us who understood not a single word of it, for the kindly face and friendly manner of the preacher were themselves a sermon. It was delivered *extempore*, and was rather a fatherly chat than a sermon. All the time he was addressing us he clasped in his hands the brass crucifix, and when he closed his remarks he held it out whilst one by one the congregation stepped forward, kissed it, and filed out.

One of our officers told me a pleasing story about this priest. The night of our arrival Captain E. E. Pearson, the first to enter his dormitory, was welcomed by a dark, bearded figure in a white nightshirt, who sprang out of bed, ran towards him, and greeted him with both hands. It was the Russian priest. He was but typical of his countrymen in his pleasure at seeing us.

Perhaps the privilege most looked forward to was the weekly bath, in a room containing four lying-down baths adjoining the chapel. At first it was open daily to all comers. A long queue of would-be bathers, with towels round their necks, was to be seen continually in those days, waiting to force themselves in as vacancies occurred. The cold weather made this tedious, and the impatient came off badly. Then a slate was hung up in the bathroom and a roster kept. Eventually certain days were allotted to different blocks of buildings, and later still to nationalities. Monday according to the last-mentioned arrangement was "British" day. It was often possible for pushing natures to get an extra bath on other days. This was effected by a judicious use of what is called "palm-greasing" in the following poem, which gives a vivid picture of what used to be a familiar scene. The poet is a subaltern, evidently steeped in the writings of Rudyard Kipling:

K.G.[1]

(With apologies to M.I.)

"I wish me mother could see me now with a towel under me arm,
Trying to get an extra tub by greasing the bathman's palm.
If she saw the soap in a 'baccy box, how very pleased she'd be.
    We used to talk of Turkish once,
      Haman, Savoy, and the Bath Club once,
      Electric, pine, and needle once,
But now we are K.G.

"The things I've got me feet stuck in would give poor Maxwell fits,
And I don't suppose they'd take my coat in the summer at the Ritz.
And my trousers haven't got the crease I always used to see:
    We used to keep 'em in presses once,
      Wetted and petted and ironed once,
      Used 'em instead of a ruler once,
But now we are K.G."

We had not been at Burg more than ten days before the order came that we were to be divided into four almost equal parties, one to remain in Burg, the other three to go to Halle and to two camps at Magdeburg. Breakfast that morning was at 6.30, because an early start had to be made by those who were leaving. It was hardly light when they fell in by "fours," laden in the now familiar fashion, the guard on either side. Amidst a great deal of confusion, shouting, calling of the roll and counting of heads three-quarters of our number left the camp. It seemed impossible for our guardians to do anything calmly and without fuss.

The parting was a sad one. Most of us had now been three months together at close quarters, and it was not easy to snap the cord which had bound us so

---

[1] *N.B.*—"K.G." means *Kriegsgefangener; i.e.* "Prisoners of War."

70 IN THE HANDS OF THE ENEMY

long as brothers in adversity. There was no cheering but a good deal of cordial handshaking, as our comrades marched away, not knowing whither they were going or what experiences lay before them.

VIII.—BURG : SETTLING DOWN

AFTER the departure of our friends there was a " general post " among those who remained. At first I was located to a room occupied by Colonel Gordon, Major Nutt, R.F.A., Major Barlow, Hampshire Regiment, Captain Maclean of Ardgour and Lieut. G. F. Connal Rowan, A. and S. Highlanders, and five or six Russian officers. My stay was a short one. After lunch the bell rang, followed by three slow strokes—the signal for a parade out of doors. We were informed that 200 French officers and 100 Belgians were expected that evening, in place of the British and Russians who had left, and that there was there and then to be what the French called a *mélange*; in other words, an intermingling of nationalities in each dormitory. On first thoughts we not unnaturally imagined that this was another attempt to stir up strife between us and our Allies, but more probably the object in view was to treat all nationalities alike, and thus prevent any one nation from complaining of worse treatment than the others. Now we knew why our family party had been broken up.

Once more it was amusement and not annoyance that could be read on every British countenance; particularly on those of the " Fenians," or inhabitants of the Irish room, who were exempted from the move. The latter seemed to survey the proceedings in the courtyard as a diversion which they would not have missed even at the price of liberty itself. There was the same kind of fuss and shouting to which we had grown accustomed, the same arranging and re-arranging, counting and counting over again. The stern calmness, said to be characteristic of the great German race, was a trait which we had seldom seen in the officers placed over us hitherto, though it was often met with in their subordinates.

To take a typical room when all was eventually settled, Major A. R. Bayly, R.F.A., Lieut. Connal Rowan, and I found ourselves the companions of four Russian and four Belgian officers who had already arrived, and of twelve French officers who were due that night. The room allotted to us was over the chapel, and was a very comfortable one if somewhat crowded. We selected our beds geographically, *i.e.* British in one nook (near the windows!), the Russians in another, and the Belgians in a third. There was nothing exclusive of course in this arrangement; it was a perfectly natural one in the circumstances, considering that as yet we were strangers to one another.

At about 10 P.M., whilst we were undressing, in trooped the French. A hearty welcome was in store for them, such as we ourselves had received eleven days previously on the night of our arrival. It was all the more cordial since they came from Torgau, and we met as friends. My old companion, Lieut. Sarraz-Bournet, with whom I had had so many walks and talks at Torgau, was of the number. A cup of soup, a pair of sausages, and a slice of bread formed their supper. Then they selected their beds and went to sleep.

The next morning after breakfast again the bell sounded, followed this time by two strokes, which meant—"back to your rooms with all speed." After a while the Adjutant came in with two or three of the staff. We all stood to attention at the foot of our cots. He politely saluted, and said to me, "Stay where you are." The remaining occupants of the room were bidden to fall into two lines. He then conducted them to their cots according to a pre-arranged scheme, which was that the three British, four Belgian, and four Russian officers were to be sandwiched in between the twelve Frenchmen. No two officers of the same nationality were to be permitted to sleep in adjoining beds. The purpose of this plan it is useless to conjecture, unless it was to annoy us by separating friends. As a fact it had precisely the opposite effect. Each of us was keen to become a "polyglot"; in other words, to be able to engage in the Babel of conversation which was carried on in the room in at least four different languages. We were now thrown together in the most convenient form, and were drawn closer in friendship by this enforced contiguity. In the room next to ours this arrangement had been already carried out by the spontaneous wish of the allied officers there.

Whether the new scheme was universally popular or not, there was little time to brood over it. On the morrow again sounded that inevitable bell. A pause. Three strokes. "Fall in outside." This was the first order issued by a new Commandant who had just taken over the reins of office. The parade which ensued was no doubt an imposing sight: the British on the right of the line, then the French, the Belgians, and the Russians. We were then formed into fours, and "right-turned." The Commandant, with interpreters on his right and the Adjutant on his left, stood facing us, about twenty paces away. On the word being given we stepped out one by one according to seniority, stood smartly to attention in front of the Commandant, saluted, told him our name, rank, and regiment, saluted again, and then marched off to a short distance behind him.

This ceremony took a long time, and was not without its humiliating aspects, had we been on the lookout for them, but we preferred, as always, to see the amusing side, and on the whole we derived considerable diversion from it.

The new Commandant was a tall, well-made, soldierly figure. He had a strong face, curiously resembling an owl. He moved about with a rapid step, followed by his satellites, and he had the authority of a god as he inspected the guard and received salutes. We were given a friendly hint that he valued a salute above all things. Although we humoured him in this respect as

THE COMMANDANT AT BURG

BURG: SETTLING DOWN

punctiliously as we knew how, it did not suffice. A notice was soon posted up explaining the proper way to salute according to German regulations, which is as follows: "Five paces before you reach the officer you are about to salute you will raise the hand to the brow. You will retain it in that position until you have reached the distance of two paces beyond that officer." When we explained that it was contrary to British custom to salute when bareheaded, an order was issued that caps must always be worn when walking in the court.

I may perhaps be allowed to relate a story about the new Commandant, particularly as it tells against myself. On the occasion of his first inspection of the rooms there was great excitement, fear, and trembling on the part of his staff. The turn of our room came. Loud altercations heralded the approach of the cavalcade as it reached the passage that leads to the room. Now there was a huge tub of stale, dust-covered water standing outside the door in case of fire. The Commandant caught sight of it. His eyes flashed lightning and his voice pealed thunder. The tub was to be emptied and refilled immediately, if not sooner; and the Commandant resumed his inspection. The door opened. A German soldier shouted out, in a voice that echoed down the now silent passage, "*Achtung!*" ("attention"). No need for such a warning. Every officer was standing as stiff as a wax-work at the foot of his cot. When the dignified figure of the Commandant entered, right hands were raised to the position of the salute, which he courteously acknowledged.

The eye which a moment ago was like a flash of lightning was now the keen eye of an eagle. In a moment of time he saw all that there was to see, nodded when he was pleased, and fumed when he saw an untidy spot. As he passed me I saluted, and then resumed a "stand-easy" attitude, the civilian within me for the moment overcoming the military. He turned round, and I was soon standing *un*easy. The eagle became the lightning once more, and the thunder boomed. He addressed me for about a minute, in tones calculated to reach me if I had been as many hundred yards as I was feet distant from him. Not a syllable did I understand, but the interpreter summed it up in a sentence: "When the Commandant is present you must stand at attention." My room-mates were highly entertained by this little episode.

It is pleasant to add that this new Commandant was in one respect just the man that we needed. From his first day he began to make the place hum, the foul clean, and in time rendered it habitable. Had there been any, he would have made the dust fly, but there was not. Indeed, the court was at first almost a bog, through which we threaded our way inch-deep in mud, and hopped over the pools. All this disappeared in a few weeks, under the Commandant's direction; the swamp was drained and the path widened. Moreover, he cleared out a shed in order to enlarge the canteen accommodation. The place really demanded such a reformer; soft and gentle methods would have been unavailing. Besides all this, his tone towards us entirely changed. He was a Judge by profession and had come across prisoners before, but in time he learnt to place us in a different category. As for myself, eventually he granted me certain facilities for carrying on my work outside the *Lager* which he might easily have refused, and when, five months later, we parted, it was with a certain measure of mutual cordiality.

The Adjutant too we soon ceased to dislike so strongly. At first he adopted an overbearing attitude and addressed us in loud and peremptory tones. Colonel Jackson explained to him in German that he would accomplish his objects more effectively by gentler methods, and he promptly followed the advice. The fact is that the German temperament is as fervid and emphatic as ours is deliberate and calm. The louder the volume of sound, the less attention did we usually pay to the words uttered. In time we grew accustomed

BURG: SETTLING DOWN

to that national trait, and when we failed unconsciously to tone it down we ceased to mind it.

On another occasion the bell summoning us to our rooms sounded one morning at 9.30. It was accompanied by an order that all windows were to be closed. For three hours our room waited in suspense, when at length it leaked out by means of signals from other rooms that the Adjutant was coming round to relieve us of any gold and paper-money we possessed beyond 60 marks. This project was aimed especially at the French, most of whom had been taken prisoner at the capitulation of Maubeuge, and were believed to have carried away vast sums of money upon their persons. This supposition was probably correct, for quite a respectable sum was gathered in, if our room was typical. The Frenchmen's word was not sufficient. Their bedding and kit were searched, and in some cases in other rooms they were stripped and their clothes examined. The Belgians had already undergone this form of scrutiny before they had left Magdeburg. Our turn soon came. Whatever money was found with us was credited to our account in German marks, and could be drawn upon in small sums as required. Towards the end of our time at Burg all German money was called in—which involved another careful search—and little bits of tin and specially printed paper-money were given us in its place. The idea obviously was to remove from us the temptation to make use of the power of the purse in order to escape. We were searched, including this occasion, seven or eight times.

One of the searches just mentioned was carried out by certain detectives belonging to the Criminal Investigation Department in Berlin. The incident was not without its lighter sides. For example, an Irish officer, who as such might have been supposed to be free from suspicion in German eyes, seized the opportunity of searching the detective's pockets whilst his own were being searched, and succeeded in obtaining a *verboten* newspaper which he found there. Again, in one of the rooms a detective entered with a costly silver-mounted stick in his hands, but he did not carry it away with him when he left. In some mysterious manner it had disappeared.

Perhaps it is worthy of mention that, at the suggestion of my fellow-prisoners, I kept a money-box for fines. It was an ordinary "Capstan" tobacco-tin with a slot pierced in the lid. Whenever an unparliamentary expression was used, a coin for the box was the forfeit, which the speaker, urged by the soliciting of his conscience—or more likely by his friends—would with his own hand place in the box. Once I had to fine the German censor. He was engaged on a hot day in examining a very large number of packages before distributing them to their owners. He let fall in an unguarded moment the remark that it was a nuisance to have to open so many parcels—specifying the particular kind of nuisance he felt it to be. Having formerly been a bank clerk in England, he was not at a loss for the epithet which described his feelings. It came glibly enough to his lips, but unfortunately for him I overheard it, and he had to pay the penalty. He did so with a good grace. The proceeds on all such occasions were periodically handed over to the churchwardens.

One of the younger British officers proved himself a great help to me in my work as chaplain, viz. Lieut. T. L. George, Suffolk Regiment. When the war broke out, he was an undergraduate of Trinity College, Dublin, preparing for Holy Orders. He now took upon himself the combined duties of chorister, lesson-reader, verger, and curate. He was, moreover, much respected by his fellow-officers. Well, in the early days at Burg Lieut. George was twice operated upon for blood-poisoning in the little finger of his right hand, the result of a wound received at Le Cateau. Instead of improving, it steadily grew worse. The room used as a hospital was less tidy and probably dirtier than any other room in the *Lager*, affording no facilities for proper dressing, sterilising, or even for pure air. The doctor from the town visited it but rarely, and our own medical officers, though they performed the operations, were at that time denied a free hand. Consequently it was deemed wisest to ask that Lieut. George might be transferred to the hospital in the town as quickly as possible, because it was found that nothing short of an amputation would be of any use. The German doctor readily concurred. A comfortable stretcher with coverings and a hood soon arrived, and George, with a smile on his face and a cigarette in his mouth, and his right arm in a sling, bade us a cheery farewell. The patient felt the parting from his comrades to go amongst complete strangers almost as much as the thought of parting with his right-hand finger. He bore himself bravely. We wished him luck and a speedy return, and I promised to try and get leave to visit him.

A few days later when I asked the Adjutant for the necessary permission to go outside the prison gates, to my surprise he answered with a generous and sympathetic "Certainly." "When may I go?" "At once, or as soon as you are ready." It is pleasant to record this episode. A few days earlier it would have been unthinkable even to ask such a boon. It was not long before I presented myself at the office for my escort. I expected a couple of armed soldiers at the least, remembering our reception at the hands of the populace. Instead my escort consisted of Herr Kost—the friendly censor and interpreter—and a soldier. "Are you going to run away?" asked Herr Kost. I smiled at the futility of such an idea. "Then we won't take the soldier."

> "How kind that little candle throws his beam!
> So shines a good deed in a naughty world."

Herr Kost will stand out in my memory as such a candle; he too was a "little" one, being short of stature, but the kind turns which he did for us showed that he had a large heart.

The doors opened, and we went out. No surly guard was there with bayonets fixed, and no angry populace throwing venomous gibes. It was a moment worth waiting for during three and a half weary months. Some of my comrades had a fear for my safety, nevertheless there was not one of them who did not envy the privilege. "I think *I* must sport a Red Cross on my arm," said a good-humoured Highlander. "I depend more upon my white collar than upon my Red Cross," I replied; and the aspersion had a regrettable basis of truth beneath it. Not always had the brassard inspired respect in our experience as prisoners. But let that pass; on this occasion it did. My journey of half an hour to the hospital, my reception there, and my return to the prison were unmarred by any unpleasant incident whatever.

The hospital was of the latest and best. Lieut. George had nothing but words of gratitude about the doctors and nurses. The amputation had indeed been performed, and he was lying weak from its effects, but uncomplaining and cheery as ever. Four days after the operation—the third time he had been under chloroform in ten days—he was compelled to walk back to the *Lager* with his right hand in a sling and his luggage in his left, with canvas shoes on his feet, and nothing on his head. A lace became untied, and the German orderly who escorted him stood and coldly watched him trying in vain to tie it, and refused to lend a hand. Though he said nothing about it, this must have been a trying ordeal to one in his state.

Throughout our stay at Burg the thanks of everyone were due to Captain E. W. Gower, Royal Munster Fusiliers, who took upon himself the duties of postman. These included the delivery of letters after they had been censored, and of the small printed slips of paper announcing parcels. We were under a like obligation to Lieut. C. H. West, Royal Dublin Fusiliers, who used daily to translate from the German newpapers all the items of general interest for the benefit of those who could not read them in the original.

The chapel, which has been described in the last chapter, had by now become a beautiful and unique sanctuary. At the far end, as you entered, stood the French altar, raised above the ground on a platform, and adorned with a frontal which had been lent to the priest by our churchwardens. Above it were hung three sacred pictures, painted by a clever French artist, Capitaine Vaugarni. Against the opposite wall was our own altar, made out of three small tables placed together, and furnished with some beautiful church fittings which had been sent out by the S.P.G., S.P.C.K., the Central Guild of Church Art at the request of Miss Gurney of the S.P.G., in addition to the lace-edged altar cloth presented by Prebendary Swayne. On the right hand stood the altar of the Orthodox Church. It consisted of a single small table entirely draped in green, with an edging of gold braid and a cross of the same material. Behind it, nailed to the wall as a dossal, hung a magenta curtain, with a large gold-braided cross standing out prominently upon it. Thus we had the three great branches of the Catholic Church worshipping the one God in the same room. There were differences of ritual and language and creed, but the spirit and intention were the same.

It is impossible to exaggerate the assistance which I received in the discharge of my duties as chaplain from the churchwardens, Colonel S. C. F. Jackson, D.S.O., and Major P. H. Collingwood. The former succeeded Colonel R. C. Bond, D.S.O., and the place of the latter was taken by Major A. C. R. Nutt, when these officers were transferred to other *Lagers*. The heartiness which characterised our services was in no small measure due to the untiring labours of Lieutenant J. Younger, who became choirmaster when Captain P. C. Davy left, Lieut. and Quartermaster W. Clark, choir secretary, and the following officers who made up the choir: Majors A. R. Bayly and W. H. Barlow; Captains H. S. Jervis, A. J. H. Maclean, and V. R. Tahourdin, Lieuts. M. B. Burrows, D. W. Hunter Blair, H. L. Pelham Burn, T. L. George, J. F. H. Houldsworth, F. C. S. Macky, R. D. Moseley, H. A.

Newson, R. F. Peskett, F. A. Sampson, R. W. Stiven, and C. H. West. R. W. Stiven has since, alas, died at Mainz.

During the six months which we spent at Burg we observed the seasons of Advent, Christmas, Lent, and Easter, and of course we saw in the new year. At a service commemorating that occasion the French priest said: "I will not wish you formally a Happy New Year, but I will wish and pray that you may have the three blessings which St. Francis de Sales desired for a friend and correspondent. They are '*Santé, Sagesse,* and *Sainteté*'" (Health, Wisdom, Holiness). After enlarging on each of these words, he turned round, and pointed to Capitaine Vaugarni's beautiful picture of our Saviour upon the cross, hanging behind the altar. "You profess," he continued, "to be followers of Him who wore a crown of thorns, but you expect to have a crown of roses."

IX.—THE REPRISAL PRISONERS

On Monday, April 12, 1915, while we were still at Burg, a leading article appeared in a German newspaper mentioning that it was proposed to take reprisals on British prisoners of war. This was on account of the solitary confinement imposed upon the captured officers and men of two German submarines who, it will be remembered, had sunk British vessels without, apparently, taking any steps to save the crews. On Tuesday afternoon the order arrived by telegram from Berlin that the following officers were to be sent to gaol: Captains R. Grey, Grenadier Guards and Royal Flying Corps, G. Elliot, Royal Irish Regiment, J. Montgomery, 7th Dragoon Guards, and the Hon. R. Keppel, Coldstream Guards, and Lieuts. the Hon. Ivan Hay, 5th Lancers, R. McLeod, R.F.A., A. D. L. Stewart, H. L. Pelham Burn, D. W. Hunter Blair, I. D. B. Hamilton, and A. W. M. Robertson, Gordon Highlanders, B. W. Allistone, Middlesex Regiment, and C. F. ffrench, Royal

STUDIES IN HEADS

From the top downwards: a typical Russian, Frenchman, Englishman, Belgian (*garde civique*), and German.

THE REPRISAL PRISONERS

Irish Regiment. As Lieut. Pelham Burn was laid up with influenza at the time, and was pronounced by the medical officer unfit to travel, all the subalterns and most of the captains volunteered to take his place. In the end Captain H. A. Cartwright, Middlesex Regiment, was selected.

The above-mentioned officers were given a few minutes to pack up, and then were taken to a room apart to be searched. Meanwhile some 400 officers had gathered in the court to witness their departure. The whole incident seemed to be regarded as a huge joke. Captain Jervis caused much amusement by taking out his handkerchief and pretending to shed copious tears. The Commandant thought it necessary to clear the court, and to this end drew up a dozen men of the guard in a long line and marched them forwards. This had the effect of huddling us together in a little crowd. His next move was to cause the bell to be rung ordering us to our rooms.

When the "reprisals" again appeared after their search and were marched under escort to the gateway, a rousing cheer went up from the officers of all nationalities who crowded the windows of every room. That was the last the majority of us saw of their friends for seven weeks. Eight of them were taken to the gaol in Burg, the rest to Magdeburg gaol.

The Commandant was extremely annoyed when he heard the cheering. We fully expected to learn that we should be punished, and so indeed it proved. On the following day a notice in Russian, French, and English appeared on the board to the effect that: "The behaviour of the officers, prisoners of war, when the British officers were led away to gaol, was earnestly to be blamed. From that day onward beer and wine would no longer be on sale until further notice."

About a fortnight later, when the American Ambassador was with us on a visit of inspection I obtained through him permission to visit the "reprisal" officers for Divine Service twice a week. With a German under-officer as escort and censor, I paid my first visit on May 2, a Sunday, to the officers confined in Burg gaol. A walk of twenty-five minutes through the continental streets of Burg brought us to the prison door. It was a small door opening out of a high wall. A few steps led us up to the warders' quarters. Mounting the stairs to the first floor, we came to a long corridor with cells on either side. A warder, keys in hand, opened one of the doors and out stepped the Hon. Ivan Hay, smiling and in the best of spirits. "The privacy of this little room," he remarked, "is preferable to the liberty and Babel of the Burg dormitories"; and as he said this he conducted me inside. It was an ordinary prison cell, about fourteen feet by seven feet, and contained a table, a chair, a locker, and a bed folded up and locked against the right-hand wall. At the far end was a window with fogged glass, the upper part opening downwards on hinges. Near the door was a stove. He had his belongings neatly arranged, and had evidently been engaged at his weekly home letter, for his writing materials were spread out upon the table.

We were soon joined by the officers of the Church of England denomination, who were Captain Cartwright and Lieuts. Hunter Blair, Robertson, Hamilton, and McLeod. The Hon. Ivan Hay was a Presbyterian, but elected to join us at the proposed service. After an exchange of greetings in the corridor, the warder and censor led the way to the chapel, which was at one end of the corridor and equal in space to about four cells. While the officers were taking their places I robed in the corridor. The chapel was a pleasant little sanctuary with a bare wooden altar, which was surmounted by a gradine, or super-altar, fitted up according to Lutheran rites with a crucifix and two (empty) candlesticks. In the tiny nave there was a harmonium, and a little aisle divided the four rows of wooden pews. The seating accommodation was about twenty. Our proceedings were watched not unsympathetically by the warder, who, however, did not understand a word of English, and by the censor, who, overcome by the walk, was soon fast asleep. We sang two hymns, "For Absent Friends" and "Abide with me," and the service was Evensong. My short address was on the text, "Be strong in the Lord," Ephes. vi. 10. The service was very hearty and reverent.

When the service was over we assembled again in the corridor to pass on our respective news, when the considerate warder allowed us to return to the chapel (which during the week did duty as a cobbler's workshop) and continue our chat there. We were permitted to talk freely, being left entirely to ourselves. The Roman Catholic officers now joined us, Lieuts. ffrench and O'Malley. These two officers said that they preferred the *Lager* as a place of internment, but the others were unanimous in their preference for the common gaol. For the first fortnight they had not been allowed to speak to one another or to smoke, but after the American Ambassador's visit these restrictions were removed. From the chapel windows we looked down upon the court where they took their daily exercise from 9 till 10 A.M. and from 4 till 5 P.M. It was 53 yards square, with grass in the centre and bounded by a flagged path. A similar path divided it from corner to corner in the shape of the capital letter Z.

It was an ordinary prison, and there were criminals in it (besides themselves!), one of whom was serving a sentence of five years. Our officers and the criminals did not meet, their intervals for exercise being at different hours.

On the following Wednesday I paid my second visit to the prison to celebrate Holy Communion, in company with the French priest who wished to see the Roman Catholic officers. We started off at 8.15 A.M. It was a glorious Spring morning, and yet there was something depressing as we walked along with our escort of two German soldiers, for almost every window displayed a flag. The previous evening a report had been circulated in the local papers that there had been a great German victory over the Russians, which included the capture of 160,000 prisoners, 400 guns, 5000 horses, and 141 motor cars. Hence the bunting and the ringing of church bells.

On reaching the prison, the first cell to be opened was Lieut. O'Malley's, who was sitting on his bed reading a newspaper. "All this news is lies!" was the cheery greeting he gave me. There was a touch of Irish exaggeration in the word "all," but the report did indeed prove to be substantially false. The total number of prisoners was reduced to 50,000, and the number of guns to sixteen. The local newspapers were justly indignant at having been imposed upon.

We had a solemn little celebration that morning, followed by a chat in the court. A table was brought out, a white cloth laid upon it, and lemonade served to the two visitors. A house which abutted on the court had a flag cheerily waving in the wind in case the prisoners should feel despondent. But despondent they were not. They expressed themselves as content as it was possible to be in their circumstances, and appreciative of such attentions as the more kindly disposed of the prison staff showed towards them.

On Sunday, May 16, I was allowed to go to Magdeburg and visit the remainder of the thirteen "reprisal" officers. Viewed from the street the prison was a fine building of recent date, very like municipal buildings in England, and externally at least quite unsuggestive of a gaol. Behind the front portion of the building was a quadrangle—the exercise ground—where the leafy branches of a tree sheltered a wooden bench from the rays of the sun. Five or six storeys of prison cells looked out upon the quadrangle from little barred windows. Crossing over to a staircase which was placarded in German, "Military Detention Barracks," and ascending two flights of stairs, we came to the floor where our officers were lodged. We were taken to a small room which was furnished with two tables, a pile

THE REPRISAL PRISONERS 85

of "biscuits" (soldiers' mattresses), and a chair. Whilst I was robing for service the officers began to come in, each carrying a stool. I did not know exactly who they would be in addition to the officers who had gone there from Burg, but as it proved they were with one exception old friends. This was Lieut. C. G. Goschen, Grenadier Guards. The others were Captains H. F. Spence and the Hon. R. Keppel; Lieutenants the Master of Saltoun, B. W. Allistone, A. D. L. Stewart, C. G. Graves, and A. F. Graham Watson. As the time at our disposal was no more than twenty minutes we cut short the warm salutations and handshakes and began the service.

We utilised the time taken in disrobing at the close of the service by jabbering away at a great rate. They had much to tell me and more to ask. In particular they were keen to learn the conditions under which the officers at Burg gaol were living, and they had messages for their friends. I visited Captain Elliot in his cell as he was unable, owing to influenza, to attend the service. Captain R. Grey also sent a message that he wished to see me in his cell. The cells were about fourteen feet by five, and were furnished with a bed, a stool, and a small shelf or bracket which served as a table. Captains Grey, Spence, and Elliot had slightly larger cells. All the officers seemed to be bearing up with soldierly fortitude, and made light of their trying lot.

I longed to be able to spend another half hour with them, but trains wait for no man, and I had to hurry off. At a later stage I had three or four other opportunities of visiting them, and of making the acquaintance of the other officers confined there (including Captain B. G. Jolliffe, Scots Guards, and Lieutenants Campbell, R. Horse Guards, and T. J. Teeling, K.O.S.B.), but this was after I had left Burg to be transferred to Magdeburg.

It should be explained that the officers specially selected were those who were known to have relatives of distinction in England. Those who themselves bore titles were the first to be chosen. This method of selection hit one of our number rather hard, Lieut. Baron W. Allistone, whose Christian name the German authorities mistook for his title.

X.—ON PAROLE

AFTER we had been six months at Burg it occurred to the German authorities, towards the end of May, that we deserved a better place of residence. So we received orders to pack up and prepare to travel to Mainz, on the Rhine. At the last moment I was bidden to take down my luggage from the baggage wagon, for I was to remain behind. For the next week I had the whole camp to myself, with the exception of two Russian soldiers who kept me company, although we could not speak each other's language.

The German Commandant took pity on my loneliness and offered me the privilege of going into the town where and when I liked, if I would give my word of honour that I would make no attempt to escape. I agreed to the proposal. We shook hands over it, put it down in writing, and he presented me with a passport for the period of a week. The feeling almost akin to freedom after seven months of internment made me feel a boy again. Hitherto, our walking space had been 160 yards by 30 yards, much smaller than an ordinary school playground.

It was evidently holiday time for me, so I lost no time before going out to explore the town. It was a queer sensation to be at large in a German town without a German escort. I soon discovered that it was holiday time also for the children, and I had not gone far before I had a following of about twenty-five boys and girls, who seemed delighted to see someone dressed in khaki, because of the fun which they thought they were going to get out of me. Two or three of them walked along

ON PAROLE

with me, and the rest followed closely on our heels. They behaved extraordinarily well, and made no offensive remarks; I am quite sure of that, because my limited knowledge of German covers all such words; I had heard them so often in the early days of our captivity. For a time I was equally pleased to see them. But I was the first to tire of the diversion, and when I thought it was time to part company I hit upon what I considered to be a happy way of accomplishing this object. We passed a sweet shop. I stopped to buy some sweets. I distributed them amongst my escort and made signs to the effect that now our ways were about to part. Not a bit of it. On the contrary, our numbers swelled at every corner which we passed down the main street.

Then another happy thought occurred to me. I would call on the Pastor. The biggest boy in the throng stepped forward and strode in front to show the way. Arriving in front of the door, he pointed to the bell which I rang. A maid answered it, but my strange appearance—an *Engländer* in khaki—was not a sufficient passport into the drawing-room. She left me on the doorstep, shut the door, and summoned her master. His Reverence was a middle-aged man in ordinary lay attire and with a kindly face. I addressed him in French and presented my pass. At once he invited me into his study and we had a chat for about ten minutes. It was a tame affair, for he could not speak English, I could not speak German, and neither of us was too fluent in French. So, after an interchange of friendly remarks, during which I calculated that my contingent of boys and girls would have an excellent chance of retiring to their homes, I bade him adieu.

Meanwhile, my young friends had entirely neglected their opportunity. There they were, as numerous as before, some sitting patiently on the doorstep, some on the kerbstone, others standing about in the middle of the road, and all of them ready to fall in the moment I appeared on the scene. It was now drawing near to tea time, so our procession wended its way to a café in the heart of the town. To my great relief it was empty of customers. Consequently, I had my tea in peace, except for the fact that the door was occasionally opened and a small head peeped in to make sure that there had been no escape by the back door. Indeed, these boys were born scouts. They had posted a guard behind as well as in front in order to "be prepared" for any unexpected move on my part. I did not hurry over tea, and as my young followers had no pressing engagements apparently, in the shape of home lessons or other attractions of that kind, to call them away, I again found myself at their head the moment I showed myself in the street. We exchanged smiles, and off we started.

The booksellers' shop was my next objective, and, wonderful to relate, I reached it with only two or three companions. The remainder had been dispersed by a shopkeeper who placed himself between me and the main body, whom he addressed in angry tones. Only the most daring spirits ventured to dart past him.

The coast was now clear for a walk to the outskirts of the town, where was a church which I had often seen from the windows of the mobilisation shed which had been my home for the past six months. I was curious to see what it looked like from the inside. I had not proceeded far, however, before a fresh crowd began to gather, and by the time we reached the church it far outnumbered the former crowd. The church being locked, I called upon the verger for the keys. This official looked upon me with a puzzled expression, and evidently regarded me as more suspicious than a suffragette. Not daring on his own responsibility to allow me to cross the sacred threshold, he took me, keys in hand, to the residence of the pastor of the church. The latter was out, but his wife was at home. After reading my pass and carefully looking me up and down, she decided that I was sufficiently innocent-looking to be permitted to visit the church. It was a fine building of the Lutheran denomination. The stone altar was adorned with crucifix and candles. The long chancel was screened off from the nave by means of wooden rails, in the middle of which, facing the congregation, was the reading desk. The pulpit was in the body of the church on the south side, very lofty, with a long flight of steps leading up to it, and a sounding-board above it. The pews were so constructed that the congregation faced the pulpit; those which were situated between the pulpit and chancel had their backs to the altar. At the west end was a gallery accommodating a fine organ.

After giving a small present to the verger's tiny daughter, who formed one of my guard, I returned to my lonesome little room at the prisoners' camp.

XI.—TORGAU REVISITED AND HALLE

A FEW days after the departure of my friends for Mainz I was granted permission to visit Torgau and Halle for the purpose of conducting Divine Service for the officers interned in those places. At 9 A.M. on Saturday, May 22, I was at Burg station awaiting my escort, who was a *Stellvertrater*, that is to say, a " deputy officer," usually a man of warrant rank temporarily commissioned for the time of the war. I already knew this officer, having had him once before as my conductor on a visit to Magdeburg. A schoolmaster by profession, he proved a civil and pleasant companion, and able to speak French. The Adjutant had sent my luggage on beforehand to the station by the Russian orderlies. I found it waiting for me; but my companion I found not. The train came in, and passed on its way without us. There was nothing to be done but go back and report myself. It appeared that the *Stellvertrater* had overslept himself. Shortly afterwards he arrived and apologised profusely. I assured him that it was all the same to me which train we caught so long as we reached our destination. But the Commandant took a different view, and told him what he thought of him in a few well-chosen words which I could hear, although I was a long distance off.

Shortly before 12 noon we took a train which caught the same connexion at Magdeburg as we should have joined had we started at the earlier hour. In the railway carriage was an under-officer, returning to the Western front after a fortnight's leave. Beside him was his young wife, not more than twenty years of age, whose eyes were red at the thought of parting with her loved one, and who fondled his hand lovingly most of the journey. As he could speak English, we chatted in a friendly manner, and by way of expressing sympathy I showed them the photo of my own wife and children which I carried in my breast pocket. There were two other soldiers in the carriage, but the majority of the passengers were Whitsuntide excursionists.

Torgau station recalled unhappy memories of that anxious morning, September 4, when I had first arrived there with the remnants of the 4th Field Ambulance, hungry, tired, and laden with a heavy pack. A spiteful crowd was waiting then to insult us with angry words and cowardly actions. But now it was different. I passed through the passengers almost unnoticed, and instead of being marched by armed Germans to the fortress, I conducted one thither myself—for my *Stellvertrater* lacked the advantage which I had had of a three months' residence in that town. This was his first visit, so he placed himself in my hands. I beckoned to a couple of boys to carry my luggage, and off we went. Not only were the conditions different, but I varied the route. I wished to buy flowers for the altar, so we made for the region of the best shops and ordered the flowers to be sent on after us.

The difference between past and present was still more marked when we reached the fortress, where the Assistant-Commandant met me with a cordial welcome. He spoke in English, and placed his office at my disposal as a bedroom. This was none other than one of the three small rooms which the mess I used to belong to had occupied in the old days. But instead of four or five mattresses laid out on the floor and two bedsteads one over the other, there was now a polished floor, a handsome table, and a bowl of flowers.

The greatest change of all was in the numbers and personnel of the fortress. When we left in November our totals exceeded 1000 French and 200 British. Now there were only about 800 French, Russian, and Belgian officers, and eighteen British, including three orderlies.

It being supper-time, I was taken to one of the large huts which had been built during our previous sojourn in Torgau. Here all the officers took their meals together, instead of at separate messes in the passages of the main building, which was the rule in our day.

The two canteens existed no longer. In their place a large wooden building had been erected near the gymnastic appliances, in appearance somewhat like a Soldiers' Institute in England. Tables and chairs were standing out in the open, at which light refreshments were obtainable. Half a dozen of us sat at one of these tables when supper was over, discussing the alteration in our circumstances, which we all agreed was a change for the better. About half of the officers had been like myself in Torgau before, having been transferred thither from Magdeburg, the other half I met now for the first time.

After a cup of coffee at the canteen we adjourned to the upper chamber in one of the sheds, which formerly some of us had known so well as St. Luke's Chapel. It had since become the Russian place of worship. The pews and altar platform, which we had built with so much trouble, had been removed. The room was now quite bare, except for an altar draped in white calico and a curtain of the same material behind it reaching from the roof to the floor.

Our Russian Allies had courteously placed this chapel at our disposal. We proceeded to deck it out

92 IN THE HANDS OF THE ENEMY

with our own ornaments. These included the frontal which Col. Bond had worked for St. Luke's, the flower vases, and the altar linen which kind friends in England had sent out for that very building, as already mentioned, but which had reached us too late ever to be used there. Thus we were quite ready for the morrow, which was Whit Sunday. Captain W. L. Dugmore, Cheshire Regiment, a Roman Catholic officer, came in while we were engaged in the work of preparation, to offer his services as organist and to report that the French priest had lent us his harmonium. An officer of the Cameronians, who was a Presbyterian and had taken a leading part in the preliminaries for the service, asked whether he might, in the absence of the ministrations of his own Church, be allowed to partake of Holy Communion with us, and of course his request was readily granted.

Sunday opened with a celebration of the Holy Communion at 6.30 A.M., which was attended by the officers and orderlies with hardly an exception. It was a peaceful little service, but we did not forget our comrades who were "in the midst of strife" nor our relatives in their more stately churches at home. Some of us, too, thought of the friends who had so often united with us in worship in that very spot, and who were now scattered in various parts of Germany. Some of the officers present told me that they had not been to a service since they had left England in August.

At 10.30 A.M. we had Matins. Colonel H. McMicking, D.S.O., Royal Scots, read the lessons, Captain Dugmore played the harmonium, and I gave a short address on "The Fruit of the Spirit is Love, Joy, Peace."

Captain Glass, Middlesex Regiment, was my host at breakfast. We had it at a table in the corner of the large hut in which he lived, and he himself was the cook. This hut, like all the others in the larger compound and the rooms inside the fortress, was shared by officers of the four allied nations.

After service I went to the Detention Barracks in

the town where Lieut. Colin Campbell, A. & S. Highlanders, one of the "reprisals," was living in solitary confinement. He had a cell to himself, but it might more accurately be described as a room. It had a couple of windows looking on to a grass courtyard and a garden, and was comfortably furnished. Compared with that of the officers in Burg and Magdeburg gaols, his lot, although so lonely, was an earthly paradise.

I had tea with Captain J. H. Knight-Bruce, R. Warwickshire Regiment, whom we had left behind sick in November, and had been at Torgau ever since. Lieut. J. Hammond, Royal Marines, told us the story of his capture at Antwerp and early imprisonment in cells, a story which was sad enough to bring tears to the eyes and cruel enough to make the blood boil. Meanwhile playing tennis in the large court was Captain H. Harrington, W. Yorkshire Regiment, a fellow-undergraduate with me twenty years ago. Time had been at work upon us both in the interval, and although we had been together at Torgau before, we had failed to recognise each other until now.

At 5 P.M. my escort took me off to the station to catch the train for Halle. Before I left, the Commandant asked me to put down in writing that during my visit I had found the officers content with their treatment. I declined to do this, and offered three reasons for my refusal. In the first place, it was contrary to regulation for anyone holding the King's commission to write anything without permission that might be used in the Press. Secondly, I could make no such general statement without going round to each officer individually and asking, Are you content? And thirdly, because even so it would convey a false impression. The Torgau officers were, it was true, more content than any others whom I had met, but if I complied with his request it might be inferred that all British officers interned in Germany were content, which at that time at any rate was by no means the case.

A two hours' journey brought us to our destination.

Pte. Boothroyd, Cheshire Regiment, with a German escort, met us at the station to carry the luggage. It was about a quarter of an hour's walk through the town to the prisoners' *Lager*, which was a large factory yard approached from one of the main streets. Passing through a high fence of barbed wire I recognised several old friends, who gave me an exceedingly hearty welcome. We had not seen one another for six months. The factory yard afforded a walking space about double the size of the court at Burg, but of the two the latter was perhaps preferable for it was on the outskirts of the town, almost in the country, whereas this yard suffered from its proximity to the town. The din of carts and trams could be heard, and the dust of the streets could be seen and inhaled. On either side of the yard were high buildings, and the windows of the neighbouring houses overlooked it. At the far end it opened out into a somewhat wider space where games could be played. Notice boards inscribed "Halt" warned the venturesome not to go too far, and numerous sentries were posted to see that the injunction was obeyed.

The dining-hall was a huge building with a cobbled floor, and a pair of rails down which in the factory days trolleys used to run. The sound of machinery was now still, but the noise of 500 human voices busily discussing a meal was heard instead. The officers had divided themselves up at little tables according to nationalities and regiments. At one of the tables was the mess of the Suffolk Regiment, who acted throughout the visit as my kind hosts. They had a spirit-lamp at hand, and a larder well filled with dainties from home. In addition to the Suffolks who had been at Torgau and Burg was Lieut.-Colonel W. B. Wallace, who had been captured within the fortnight previous to my visit. There were other fresh faces, including Lieut.-Colonel S. H. Enderby and four or five officers of the 5th Fusiliers, some Territorials, and a few naval officers.

At 6.30 next morning I met a large part of the

British contingent at the shower-bath, which inasmuch as it had a dressing-room attached to it was superior to the douche which had latterly been erected at Burg. Among them was my old friend Captain E. E. Pearson, Suffolk Regiment, the handy man who had done so much in the building of St. Luke's Chapel at Torgau. He had made every preparation for my visit as far as church services were concerned. Indeed he had been in the habit of conducting a service every Sunday himself in the absence of a chaplain. Occasionally a German professor from Halle University had given the British officers a service, but as a rule they had been dependent upon Captain Pearson, assisted by Major A. S. Turner, Royal Berkshire Regiment, as lesson-reader, and a Territorial officer as pianist, whose name I cannot recall.

Captain Pearson now helped me to prepare for a service at 8.30 A.M. We extemporised an altar in a small reading-room. At the hour mentioned it was filled to overflowing by about thirty-five officers. Others found standing-room at the door and round the windows. After Matins, with two or three hymns sung with much heartiness, came a celebration of the Holy Communion for which nearly all the congregation remained.

Then came breakfast, followed by an inspection of the sleeping rooms. The one occupied by Captain Pearson was immediately above the dining-hall, from which it was approached by a flight of stairs. It was more like a loft than a dormitory, but it had been made as comfortable by the occupants as circumstances permitted. The other rooms which I visited were long, narrow, low, and crowded. Four of the most senior officers had a comparatively luxurious room to themselves in a house near the entrance to the *Lager*. It was lofty, and furnished with every convenience which they could reasonably desire. These fortunate officers were Colonels Enderby and Wallace, Major Peebles and another. The sanitary arrangements were the best of any internment-camp I had yet visited.

The day of my visit proved to be very hot. Most of

the officers were sitting about the yard in hammock chairs, some chatting, some reading, and practically all smoking. Amongst the cheeriest and bravest of all was Captain R. W. Thomas, Royal Munster Fusiliers, who had now been deprived for nearly eight months of the power of speech. Other officers were strolling up and down. And some who wished for a more violent form of exercise were playing Rounders at the wider end of the yard.

The orderlies of all nationalities were accommodated in a long and narrow upstairs room. Some of our men had picked up a smattering of French and German. All were full of good humour and in excellent health. The names of the British orderlies were: Ptes. H. Robinson, A. Boothroyd, and T. Shannon (Cheshire Regiment), and W. Webster (Norfolk Regiment). Their smart appearance was well calculated to give the Germans a favourable impression of the British soldier.

At the station I asked two Red Cross ladies to give the two men who carried my luggage a cup of coffee, which they did very graciously, presenting each of them at the same time with a cigar. I told the ladies that their kindness was much appreciated, and would be set against a less happy memory of the Red Cross officials on our first journey as prisoners of war.

Extra editions of the evening papers were being distributed at the station, consisting of a one-page leaflet which contained Italy's declaration of war and Austria's and Germany's replies to it.

On reaching Burg I met the Commandant upon the road, who broke the news to me that I was to be transferred to Magdeburg on the morrow.

XII.—MAGDEBURG

On the morning following the events related in the last chapter the *Stellvertrater* met me at Burg Station and travelled with me to Magdeburg, a distance of twenty

THE WAGENHAUS, MAGDEBURG

The long low shed to the left of the Wagenhaus is the chapel, the smaller shed adjoining it is the dog-kennel. *Drawn by Col R. C. Bond, D.S.O., King's Own Yorks Light Infantry.*

MAGDEBURG

miles. Our arrival came as a surprise to the British officers interned there. It happened to be during the midday confinement to rooms, which took place daily from 11.45 to 1.30. Our taxi-cab was observed from the windows, and Captain F. Bell, Gordon Highlanders, met me at the door. He led me to the office (where I underwent my seventh and last search but one), and kindly made a request that I might be located to his room, which was instantly granted. The other British officer living in it was Major B. Chetwynd-Stapylton, "The Optimist," and there were besides twenty-three officers of the allied nations.

The barbed-wire enclosure which was now to be my abode for a month consisted of " Scharnhorst," a semicircular fortress similar to the one at Torgau, only much smaller, and of "Wagenhaus 9," a rectangular mobilisation shed of three storeys. The two buildings faced each other obliquely across an exercise ground of about 200 yards by 100. Each was cut off from the other by iron railings and a barbed-wire fence respectively, the gateways of which were, however, now allowed to remain open during the greater part of the day. In the early days, I was told, communication between the two places had been cut off entirely. It was to the Wagenhaus that I was located. The ground floor was unoccupied, except in one small corner which served as the guardroom. Evidently the lower portion of the building had been used for stabling horses and storing wagons. On the first floor was a long corridor with large rooms partitioned off from it which looked out upon the court. The corridor was airy, having numerous windows facing the Elbe, which flowed past at a few yards distance. There were five or six rooms along this corridor, containing from one to three British officers amongst about twenty-five of the Allies. At one end of the passage was the office, approached by a staircase on the south side of the building; at the other end the hospital room and another staircase. Both staircases led downwards to the court and upwards to the third storey. Ascending we come to a double row of rooms, one row looking out upon the court, the other upon the Elbe, and a corridor dividing them. There were when I arrived twenty-five British officers in this block, and twelve at Scharnhorst. In one of the rooms on the top floor of the Wagenhaus there were about forty orderlies of all the nationalities, including four British. There were also three British orderlies in Scharnhorst. Two German soldiers were always on guard by day as well as by night on both the corridors.

Our room contained two long rows of beds, four windows commanding a view of the court at one end, and the door at the other. My two British companions and I occupied adjoining beds—the rule about separating nationalities not being enforced here. About a fortnight after my arrival Scharnhorst was given up entirely to the Belgian officers of Flemish extraction, and the British officers who had been living there were distributed amongst the rooms in the Wagenhaus. By this arrangement our little mess gained two new members, Major P. Lowe, W. Yorks. Regiment, and Major J. A. D. Bell, A.S.C.

The chief object of attraction out of doors was the newly-made tennis court, situated in the open space between Scharnhorst and the Wagenhaus. There was no grass about it, nevertheless it was level, and a high fence of wire-netting surrounded it. The court was made by the British officers, assisted by the Allies and some German workmen. A club was formed to include all who wished to play, the subscription being seven marks. The Secretary was Lieut. Poret, who had represented France at tennis. The committee was international, comprising a member from each of the Allies; our representative was Major G. S. Tweedie, R. Scots. Every member of the club got a chance of an hour's play in doubles about once in three days. A roster containing the names of players and their hours of play was written up daily on a blackboard, and the rules were adhered to strictly, to the satisfaction of all.

MAGDEBURG

In the absence of flannels, the approved costume during the hot weather was pyjamas. During the month of June a tournament was held.

Amongst our best players were Major P. Lyster, R.F.A., Major J. A. D. Bell, A.S.C., Lieut. O. G. B. Philby and Lieut. J. C. W. MacBryan, Somerset L.I.

There was an excellent shower-bath, open, however, only from 8.15 A.M. to 9.45 A.M. It was cold except on Wednesday and Friday, when the water was hot and the time extended to 11 A.M.

The outstanding feature of the day's routine was the *Appel*—in other words, the roll-call—which took place at 8 A.M., 1.30 P.M., and 6 P.M. The officers paraded in the courtyards and were counted, first by rooms and then by nationalities, the whole process taking about twenty minutes. In addition to this, every night shortly after "lights out" (10 P.M.) a couple of under-officers visited the rooms and counted us as we lay in bed. These excessive precautions were due to the numerous but unsuccessful attempts to escape which had been made. The two medical officers, one of the medical orderlies, and myself were exempted from all roll-calls.

The Commandant, a naval officer generally known as "The Admiral," was extremely courteous in his demeanour towards us. Since he took up his duties on May 1 the conditions and general comfort had greatly improved, and the contentment of the prisoners proportionately increased. He was assisted by two captains, one at Scharnhorst and the other at the Wagenhaus. These again were each of them assisted by an adjutant. One of the adjutants, Lieut. Baron von Benningsen, a reservist cavalry officer, spoke English and French fluently. He devoted himself to ameliorating the lot of the prisoners. We were able to go to him at any moment, and, however busy he might be, he always seemed to have leisure to hear complaints and tact enough to get the causes removed.

In order fully to appreciate the difference inaugurated

by the "Admiral's" régime, it is necessary to make a passing reference to the stringency of his predecessor's rule, who was a thorough-going martinet. Signet rings and watches, for example, were confiscated, lest they should be used for the purpose of bribes. And by his order tobacco and chocolate were removed before their eyes from the officers' parcels. Another act of his was to confine fifteen officers in prison cells for playing football with a loaf of *Kriegsbrot* (war bread). The story is that an officer was crossing from the canteen to his room with the loaf, when some one pushed it from under his arm, and it fell into the snow, which lay thick on the ground. Then began the football match. It was obviously an unpremeditated prank due to the spirits of youth, and was condemned as such by the senior officers. The Commandant regarded it in a more serious light, and sentenced the players to six days in cells and the owner of the loaf to thirteen days. When every allowance is made, it must be owned that a punishment of less severity would have fitted the crime. The offenders were locked up without books, tobacco, or companionship of any kind. One of them, the unfortunate owner of the loaf, Captain W. Neish, Gordon Highlanders, described afterwards how he filled up the time. He divided up the days into periods of two hours, allotting to each a subject for meditation. Thus he visited his old home and his friends, then he reviewed the books he had read, then he lived over again the days spent in fishing and shooting, and the evenings at dances. And so the lonely time dragged along.

It has been mentioned that certain attempts to escape were made. On one of those occasions two Russian and one Belgian officer had secreted themselves in the chapel at vespers, and remained there undiscovered after the chapel had been locked up. Casting lots for the order in which to make their exit, the first two (the Russians) succeeded in squeezing through the upper part of a window. The Belgian, when it came to his turn, was unable to climb up unassisted, and was consequently left

THE COMMANDANT AT MAGDEBURG AND HIS ADJUTANT

MAGDEBURG

behind. The Russians meanwhile walked on until they reached a point within a few miles of the Polish border, where, completely exhausted, they were recaptured and brought back to the *Lager*. The Belgian seized another chance of getting away, but was apprehended close to the frontier of Denmark. Undeterred, he made yet another dash for liberty. Some artisans from the town had been at work laying the foundations of the tennis court; he quietly took possession of the pass belonging to one of them from the pocket of his coat, which was hanging up temptingly while the owner's back was turned. Armed with this the Belgian took train to the frontier, but failed to get farther than Aachen, where he was seized and put in prison. Not unnaturally the authorities, up to the time of my departure from Germany, had considered this the safest place for his internment.

One more attempt was made to escape by another Belgian, a young fellow of nineteen, the son of a distinguished statesman. One night while convalescing in the hospital room on the first floor he jumped out of the window, and alighted without injury over the barbed-wire fence on to the bank beyond it. He calmly walked along the railway line, and when challenged described himself as a civilian inspector. This worked all right until he chanced against an official, who informed him that there was no such thing, arrested him, and escorted him back to the Wagenhaus. He soon found himself in prison for a short spell. It was during his imprisonment that I arrived, and that at Captain Bell's suggestion his bed had been located to me. He used to mess at the same table with Major Stapylton and Captain Bell, where again I fell into his place. I was, however, the only inhabitant who benefited by his escapade. The rest were subjected to further restrictions of their liberty whilst the barbed-wire fences were being strengthened.

The escape from the chapel rendered it necessary to keep that building carefully guarded during service time, and securely locked at all other times. The French daily service was disallowed, and it was somewhat difficult to obtain leave for any week-day service at all. Moreover, the Sunday services for both the Roman Catholics and ourselves were limited to one hour each.

The Sunday after my arrival was Trinity Sunday. We were permitted to hold a service at 10.30, all the arrangements for which were made by Captain Bell, who was a popular officer with the powers that be. The lessons were read by the churchwardens, Lieut.-Colonel C. M. Stephenson, the senior British officer, and Lieut.-Colonel R. C. Bond, whose name is already familiar to the reader. A number of the allies, mostly Russians, who had no service of their own, were welcome members of the congregation. Lieut. Boel (Belgian), played the harmonium, and voluntaries were given by Count de Crécy (a French private soldier) on the 'cello, with harmonium accompaniment by Lieut. Rémond (French). These three officers were Roman Catholics, and rendered their assistance with the approval of the priest. The choir consisted of about fifteen British officers, whose names were, to the best of my recollection: Majors G. S. Higginson, J. A. D. Bell, and G. D. H. Ewart, Captains F. Bell, N. A. Bittleston, R. C. Campbell, A. F. Day, P. C. Nicholls, C. H. Rawdon, and W. W. Wagstaff, Lieuts. E. H. W. Backhouse, P. P. Butler, J. C. W. MacBryan, O. G. B. Philby, and J. B. Taylor. The rule of the place was that sermons must be handed in at the office, in duplicate, by the Friday evening previous to their delivery, in order to receive the office stamp as an *imprimatur;* and the preacher was expected to read from the one copy, and the censor to follow word for word from the other. The service thus described was typical of the others which were held during my stay in Magdeburg. The unfortunate French priest, a saintly white-haired man, once was sentenced to six days in cells, simply because on Joan of Arc's day he urged his congregation to pray *pour nos âmes* which a

German officer who was present misunderstood to mean *pour nos armes!*

Before my arrival a minister of the Lutheran Church, Herr Schneider, used occasionally to conduct a service for the British officers in English, which was warmly appreciated by them.

On the day of the fall of Przemysl Colonel F. Neish, Captain L. H. Josephs, Lieut. F. H. Bevan, and I visited the town under escort to see an oculist. It was a unique opportunity, for we were able to obtain the advice of a specialist of repute for the paltry sum of six marks. From the residence of the oculist we drove to an optician in order to purchase glasses in accordance with the prescriptions. During the ten minutes which elapsed before we made our reappearance in the street, a dense crowd lined the pavement, leaving a narrow passage between the door of the shop and our taxicab. Church bells were ringing, and shops and houses on both sides of the street were decked out with bunting; consequently as we ran the gauntlet, we had the happy feeling of driving off to our honeymoon. With two of us, however, this feeling was tempered by the recollection that our better halves were far away, and with the other two that their better halves had yet no existence, as such. The barbed-wire enclosure soon dispelled all such delusions, and recalled us to reality. In the case of my three companions this was the first time that they had mingled with the outside world for six months.

Looking back upon the four weeks I spent at Magdeburg, it is pleasant to recall the daily Greek Testament reading with Professor Belfour; the daily walk at 11 A.M. with Colonel Neish round and round the central court; the afternoons under a bright summer sun in company with a congenial friend or a book, the tea parties in various rooms, made possible by parcels which arrived regularly from home; and the evenings after supper when Colonel A. W. Abercrombie, Colonel F. and Captain W. Neish, Major R. A. Gray, Major G. D. Ewart, Captain J. H. Graham, and occasionally others, came to our room to hear the German newspaper translated by Major Stapylton or Lieut. P. P. Butler, and to discuss (and discount) its contents.

It is a long lane that has no turning. At length the order was announced that medical officers, hospital orderlies, and chaplains were to be exchanged. Personally I was reluctant to accept the offer and to leave my little flock unshepherded; but acting on the advice of the senior officers, it was deemed wisest that I should avail myself of an opportunity to return to the front.

On the afternoon before our departure my room mates, with that kindliness of heart which was characteristic of them, entertained the "choir boys" to tea and to bid me farewell. The same hosts invited to a sumptuous dinner cooked by themselves three or four of the officers who used to spend their evenings in our room, and the two Frenchmen whose music had brightened our Sunday services. The dinner was followed by speeches and the singing of the National Anthem—the first and only time I heard it during my ten months in Germany.

On the last day, within an hour of our departure, all the colonels, majors, and one or two senior captains, assembled in Colonel Stephenson's room for a cup of tea and to give Lieut. Butler and myself an official send-off. Our host, in a happily-worded speech, announced that, although they were losing their chaplain, he had made arrangements that they should continue their Sunday services. He referred to the loss which the community would sustain by the departure of Lieut. Butler, and to the universal sympathy which was felt for Captain Graham, who that very morning had contracted pneumonia and was unable to travel. That unfortunate officer, instead of marching off as he hoped with his brother-officer and four orderlies for home, was carried away in an ambulance cart to hospital.

The German officers and one or two German soldiers came forward amongst our fellow-countrymen and the Allies to give us a final handshake and a cordial farewell. The last words that we heard as we passed beyond the barbed-wire were, "Don't forget to write to my wife!" and, "Don't forget the message to my mother!"

XIII.—PRISON OCCUPATIONS

OLIVER WENDELL HOLMES tells the story of a certain pin which a lady wore as a brooch. A tiny ornament, yet it had discharged a great service. And this is the history of it. Her husband was thrown into prison for some political offence. Being left to his own thoughts as his sole companions, in time these began to bore him to the pitch of insanity. No books, no visitors, no letters; only the past to live over again, and perhaps live differently, and the future without any sure prospect that he would live it at all. He was on the verge of becoming a raving lunatic when an unexpected diversion came to the rescue. He discovered upon his person a black pin. Carelessly he threw it on the floor, and then groped about until he found it. The size of the pin, its dark colour, and the dim light made this no easy task, but at last he found it. Then he lost it again, searched for it again, and found it again. An idle occupation for an idle fellow, perhaps; but it saved him from melancholia. An active mind cannot cease to revolve any more than the earth can; and it is better to revolve around something than around nothing, even if it be but a black pin. No wonder that he carried away with him that pin when he left the prison, and no wonder his wife had it set with pearls and wore it next to her heart. It had saved her husband's reason.

Prisons have been the birthplace of many works of genius. We are told that genius is akin to madness, if not an actual manifestation of it. The man with the black pin, if he had had access to pen and paper might have left a permanent mark on the world's literature.

106 IN THE HANDS OF THE ENEMY

One of the greatest historical works in the world was written while its author was in exile—" The History of the Peloponnesian War" by Thucydides. Locke was a refugee in Holland when he wrote his "Essay on the Human Understanding." These works, however, did not issue from the walls of an actual prison cell, as did the "Pilgrim's Progress" and "Don Quixote"; the one written in Bedford gaol, the other in a squalid dungeon in Spain. Sir Walter Raleigh during his thirteen years in the Tower left behind him a "History of the World" as evidence that his days were not all spent in idleness. The highest instance of all is St. Paul, who wrote some of his best-known epistles whilst in captivity.

These men had certain elements of good fortune in their seeming misfortune. They had leisure, they had inspiration and ability to turn it to account, and they had writing materials wherewith to give permanent record to their prison meditations. If they had never been to prison the world in all probability would be the poorer for the lack of these immortal books.

With the prisoners of war, in the early days of our internment the circumstances did not appear to be conducive to the creation of works of genius which the world will not willingly let die. Leisure was plentiful, but it was by no means undisturbed. Books of reference or of any kind whatever, for the first few weeks, there were none. Later on these handicaps were partially removed, and it may be that prison literature will yet see some additions to its list from the indelible pencils[1] of our prisoners of war.

At Torgau during the first month the time was spent in walking round and round a very limited court, and in talking round and round a single limited topic—how we came to be captured, and how soon we should find ourselves again at liberty. It was not anticipated that the internment would be of long duration. The prophets varied from a fortnight to three months. If

---

[1] Pen and ink were not permitted.

PRISON OCCUPATIONS 107

anyone imagined that it might last a year he had not the courage to give voice to his gloomy forebodings.

Athletic diversions were the earliest, and most natural, and probably in the circumstances the best. They took many forms, beginning with physical exercises under the direction of an expert, Lieut. C. M. Usher, Gordon Highlanders, who was also an ideal instructor. He led his pupils by graded exercises from the simple to the strenuous, and concluded each day's programme with a game. Sometimes it would be "leap-frog," sometimes "French and English," sometimes "twos and threes," and in later days Highland dances. The idea of physical exercises owed its inception to Captain C. H. Ackroyd, K.O.Y.L.I., who for the first few days acted as instructor. In the afternoon football was played. The heat of the German autumn was no discouragement to ardent spirits. Association, with extemporised goal-posts, was the usual game, and occasionally an international contest with the French would be held. On certain days in the week the English orderlies competed with the French orderlies, and nearly always beat them. Once the game peculiar to Eton College was played, the number of old Etonians being nearly enough to form the two sides.

After a while a flat piece of bare ground was marked out as a tennis court. It mattered little that there were a few humps and hollows, and no wire netting to keep the balls from wandering. This game continued to be played right into the depths of winter, until we left Torgau, and would have been resumed at Burg had there been a piece of ground available.[1] There were gymnastic appliances both at Torgau and at Burg, which were made good use of by experts and others. So much for the exercising of arms and legs.

During the long winter evenings idle fingers were made busy with knitting needles. Highlanders kept themselves supplied with stockings, and others used to

[1] The tennis court and tournament at Magdeburg have been already described.

knit their own socks, Beginners in the art contented themselves with knitting scarves. Some who had been brought up on the theory that the deft use of a needle was entirely a feminine accomplishment actually espied holes in their garments with unfeigned delight for the pleasure of patching them or darning them. Many of the darns and most of the patches, it must be owned, supported the above theory. There were, none the less, specimens of needlework and delicate fancy-work which were real monuments of masculine genius. One officer made himself a dressing-gown out of a blanket; another a coat to replace the one which he had lost on the occasion of his capture.

There were in the line of carpentry talents of no mean order, as St. Luke's Chapel at Torgau bore eloquent testimony. Lieut. J. Berry, S. Lancs. Regiment, could with the aid of a penknife and a few extemporised tools make the most hopeless watch tick again, and the abandoned fountain pen write once more.

Of indoor recreations bridge provided a pastime of which its devotees never tired. Draughts and chess filled other leisure hours. A military game called Attack was manufactured by Major W. H. Long out of cards found in cigarette boxes, and aroused considerable interest and competition amongst a certain few. At a later stage in our imprisonment picture puzzles were sent out, some of them comprising even 1000 pieces and occupying as many as four days to put together. When we had finished with them we passed them on to the Allies. Never till then did we know that silence and quiet could be so nearly approached in a crowded room. Indeed, we were sorry that kind friends at home had not thought of sending these puzzles earlier. Akin to picture puzzles were small cardboard boxes containing twelve numbered blocks of wood, which after one of them had been removed and the rest jumbled up had to be coaxed back into their proper order. In principle these antidotes to madness were not unlike the expedient of the politician and his black pin.

PRISON OCCUPATIONS

Definitely intellectual pursuits were by no means neglected, and were indulged in by those who played games and solved puzzles as well as by others for whom the latter had no attractions. At Torgau the medical officers attended lectures daily given by Dr. L. J. Austin, F.R.C.S., Registrar of the London Hospital, whose thrilling experiences as a prisoner of war

AT WORK AND AT PLAY

have been published. There was a useful pastime engaged in by several of the senior officers which kept them extremely busy for a time and helped us all, but they would not care for me to enlarge upon it.

Artists and caricaturists were in their element; their skill in this direction must have surprised themselves, and certainly it caused diversion to everyone. A touch of humour saves many a situation, and was one of the best cordials for spirits which might have become despondent or depressed. There was, to the best of my knowledge, no sort of concerted agreement on the subject, but it seemed as though every officer had resolved to take petty annoyances in the spirit of a practical joke; and the orderlies bore their confinement in the same brave spirit. Certain it was that when the German officials discovered that we were proof against minor insults they gradually ceased to perpetrate them. With all their fine qualities, a sense of humour is not a conspicuous German trait.

The number of books read and circulated was truly astonishing. At one time a bookseller used to be allowed in and erected a book-stall which only the pushing and the patient were able to get anywhere near, before its contents were disposed of. Books were obtainable in all the languages spoken, and could be ordered if the required works were not in stock. The editions most commonly seen were those of the Tauchnitz firm and Messrs. Nelsons'. The thirteen volumes of Carlyle's "Frederick the Great," the three volumes of his "French Revolution," Homer's "Iliad" and "Odyssey," in Greek and in French; Motley's "Dutch Republic," Gibbon's "Decline and Fall," Macaulay's "History" and "Essays," Buckle's "History of Civilisation," Kinglake's "Eothen," Erskine Childers' "Riddle of the Sands," Pepys' "Diary," Boswell's "Life of Johnson," Plutarch, Shakespeare, and Ruskin are a few samples of the stiffer food which braced the more energetic minds. Italian, Russian, French, Spanish, German, and Hindustani Grammars and Conversational Manuals were always in evidence, and led to a splendid *entente cordiale* between the Allies with whom the study of some of these languages brought studious officers into close contact. Shorthand in Pitman's and Sir Edward Clarke's methods each had its respective advocates and diligent students. The dead languages found enthusiasts amongst a few who had not been put off these studies in their schooldays. The number of University men from Oxford, Cambridge, and Dublin was considerable. Certain officers set themselves the task of reading the masterpieces of literature to which they were introduced through the pages of Conan Doyle's "Behind the Magic Door."

At the same time novel reading was not neglected. To read a couple of novels a day without interfering with outdoor exercise and social duties was quite an ordinary feat. In time we amassed at the various *Lagers* really respectable libraries, thanks to the efforts of Major E. H. Jones, R.F.A., Captain A. J. H. Maclean, and others. The kindness of friends at home, of the staff of the American Embassy in Berlin, of firms such as Mudie's and the S.P.C.K. deserve our special gratitude for their liberal gifts of books. One officer at least conceived the ambition to write a novel himself. On the whole, the wonderful thing was that although as a rule one day was exactly the same as another the time did not hang upon our hands; it flew by at a rate with which those who considered themselves busy found it hard to keep pace. When there was anything unusual to do it was difficult to fit it in, particularly if there was anything uncongenial about it.

Far and away the most pleasant experience we had was the receiving of parcels and letters, and next to that, if not equal to it, the pleasure of acknowledging them. The Church Army is doing a good work in sending out parcels of food, tobacco, and books for the men. The procedure in the case of the delivery of parcels was as follows. A slip of paper would be distributed to the fortunate ones, and at the time appointed they would fall into line outside the parcels-room to await their turn. They would then be called in one by one and their parcels would be opened by a censor and examined in front of them. Cakes might be cut and tins were invariably opened to make sure that they did not contain notes or cuttings from newspapers. If the various articles of food were not immediately required they could be put aside at the owner's request unmutilated, and taken out after examination when wanted. Incoming letters were delivered promptly after being censored, but letters addressed by prisoners to England were retained for ten days before they were censored and posted. At Magdeburg letters could be given in only on stated days twice a month, and they were restricted to a certain size of notepaper and to a prescribed number of lines. Postcards could be written weekly.

The foregoing narrative is written at the commencement of the second year of the war. From letters which the author constantly receives from the relatives of his former fellow-prisoners there seems to be more contentment with the treatment that they are now receiving. They are treated for the most part as officers, which cannot be said of the early days. On the score of healthy conditions and medical treatment when required, relatives of officers interned in Germany need entertain no anxiety, and still less with regard to the spirit in which they have resigned themselves to their lot. With regard to the men's camps I cannot speak from personal experience, since I was always refused permission to visit them. As to the manner in which the officers are spending their long period of enforced leisure, it is hoped that this chapter has sufficiently demonstrated that they are turning it to good account and preparing themselves for the day when their services will once more be at the disposal of their country.

www.ingramcontent.com/pod-product-compliance
Lightning Source LLC
Chambersburg PA
CBHW070500090426
42735CB00012B/2627